"*A helpful collection of simple lessons and insights designed to give women a competitive edge in one of the world's toughest—and most promising— markets.*"—John Sculley, Chairman and CEO, Apple Computer, Inc.

"*A great deal has been written in the U.S. press about Japanese women and their emerging role in their nation's business. However, Wilen and Brannen have effectively addressed an even greater problem for Western women doing business in Japan, the 'cultural' trade barriers, obstacles erected over centuries. A must read for businesswomen in any way associated with Japanese business . . . a should read for virtually all businessmen who are exposed directly or indirectly to the Japanese culture.*"—William S. Meyers, Vice President, Time Inc. Magazine Company, Publisher, *Money* Magazine

"*What* Games Mother Never Taught You *did for women in business in the 70s . . . these authors do for businesswomen of the 90s.*"—The Honorable Patricia C. Sullivan, Ed.D., San Francisco Commission on the Status of Women (affiliation for identification purposes only)

"*The ideas and information shared in the book are a tremendous tool for my visits to Japan—years of experience are at my fingertips to reference all occasions. A necessity for women who travel to Japan, offering valuable support and guidance.*"—Felitia Lee, Director, Finance, Barnes-Hind International

"*Must reading for any women involved with the world of Japanese business. Men also will benefit from the experience of these career women who have paved the way in a very difficult and demanding environment.*"—Fred Forsyth, Senior Vice President and General Manager, Macintosh Hardware Division, Apple Computer, Inc.

"*Having worked in Sony Corporation of Japan for over two years, I know when I see a good book on personal conduct for foreign women. This is it.*"— Michelle L. Long, Business Planner, Sony Corporation of America

"A remarkably enjoyable and insightful reinforcement of the dos and don'ts of any dealings with the Japanese. A valuable resource for both women and men alike."—H. Stephen Slater, Managing Director, ORBYX Global Trade Group, Inc.

"A good practical guide for the newcomer to this challenging environment, but also helpful to anyone who would benefit from a better understanding of Japanese businessmen. Very readable—the examples contribute a lot."— Barry R. Linsky, Senior Vice President, Planning and Business Development, The Interpublic Group of Companies, Inc., Worldwide Advertising and Marketing Communications

"Thank you for sharing women's first-hand experiences with Japanese business. Your book offers pragmatic solutions for the experienced businessperson as well as the novice."—Linda Lawrence, Apple Computer, Inc., Pacific Division, Office of the President

"Finally, a concise handbook that defines the rules—both hidden and obvious—for dealing with Japanese businessmen."—R.C., Sun Microsystems

"Physically, traveling to Japan can be demanding, but it is nothing compared to what a professional woman has to contend with when she comes face to face with business customs in Japan."—Glen Freeman, Smith, Steiner & Thomas, Consultants to the Travel Industry

"You don't need to take a business trip to Japan to find a use for this book. Anyone dealing in the real estate market today needs to understand the Japanese culture."—Sherry Kline, Vice President, Fidelity National Title

"An essential tool for any businessperson. Wilen and Brannen's book is well researched and genuinely useful, a sort of 'business etiquette' guide for Western women working in Japan. It will be of equal interest to all business people, however, as it includes real insights into ways to cross the cultural gulf between West and East. For example, did you know you should use the blunted end of your chopsticks to pick up 'communal' food? Sounds obvious when you hear it . . . but you'll likely hear it here first."—Nigel Brachi, Marketing Manager, Philips Electronics Ltd

"A logical and easy to read guide for anyone now doing or wishing to do business with the very uniquely styled culture of Japan. Described here is a very positive and cooperative approach to understanding the nuances of the tradition-rich Japanese that are critical in building lasting and productive relationships with our friends from the East. The success of the future will be largely dependent on our capacity to partnership with them. In the short time it takes to read this book you will learn what would otherwise cost you years in frustrating trips to Japan."—M. Laurie Bussey, Second Vice-President, American National & Trust of Chicago

"If Japanese men who read this book assimilate the message and if women who read it heed the book's advice, it will accelerate the inevitable cultural change within Japanese society of accepting professional women in the workplace. In short, this is a tremendous bridge to the cultural gap that exists in the business world today between professional working women and Japanese businessmen, and has the added benefit of improving the situation for American businessmen."—Robert Holmes, District Sales Manager, Mitsubishi Electronics America

"Every business has its own language . . . however, women have had to learn more than 'one language' in dealing with the Japanese business environment. I highly recommend this book to all my clients, but especially to women executives who travel to Japan."—Maryles Casto, Chairman and CEO, Casto Travel

"This book provides excellent practical guidance for business and professional women working with and for Japanese companies. In addition, I would also highly recommend it to men who are working on the same team with such women. First, it correctly dispels any concern whether women can be as effective as men in working with Japanese companies—they CAN! Second, there is a risk that men may overlook the crucial need, especially at the beginning of a project, to take special steps to reinforce the authority and expertise of their female colleagues who are working with Japanese counterparts. This book gives several concrete suggestions for overcoming that problem."—Michael R. Moyle, Esq., Head of the Japan Practice Group, Graham & James, Former President of The Japan Society of Northern California

Doing Business with Japanese Men

A Woman's Handbook

CHRISTALYN BRANNEN & TRACEY WILEN

STONE BRIDGE PRESS
Berkeley, California

Published by STONE BRIDGE PRESS
P.O. Box 8208, Berkeley, California 94707

Cover design by Stephanie Young.

10 9 8 7 6 5 4 3 2 1

Printed in the United States of America.

Library of Congress Cataloging-in-Publication Data

Brannen, Christalyn.
    Doing business with Japanese men : a woman's hand-
book / Christalyn Brannen and Tracey Wilen.—1st ed.
       p.   cm.
    Includes index.
    ISBN 1-880656-04-3.
    1. Business etiquette—Japan. 2. Corporate culture—
Japan. 3. Negotiation in business—Japan.   I. Wilen, Tracey.
II. Title.
HF5389.W55   1993   92-36102
395'.52—dc20   CIP

Contents

By Christalyn Brannen

DEDICATION

I dedicate this book to Rinko, Burunnen, and Orenji in appreciation and admiration—three persons who are dear to me and who now are a part of me in ways I have only recently come to know. I especially want to thank Rinko for sharing with me her life experiences and understanding of the Japanese, Burunnen for her forthrightness in relaying her confusions and insights as a young professional woman working in Japan, and Orenji most of all for her example of true courage in taking the more difficult and lonely path when coming to decisive crossroads in her life. My heart is full of memory and love and will forever be grateful for knowing you.

Many books talk about the delicate art of negotiating with the Japanese, but this is the first book to look at the uniquely delicate situation that confronts the Western businesswoman, whether she is traveling to Japan for meetings, working for a Japanese company, or hosting her clients at her home office. It is long overdue. Western women have arrived at positions of authority in business. And Japanese businessmen have shown themselves vulnerable, and in some instances even receptive to change.

I grew up in Japan. The writing of this book is thus a product of my own experiences as well as those of the women I have met and worked with in my consulting on Japan and in my seminar "Business Communications with the Japanese" (conducted over the past five years for more than thirty different companies in six different countries). The need for this book became increasingly obvious to me as I got more and more questions at my seminars directed to me from men and women on the subject of women working with Japan. At first I didn't want to treat the subject as a separate issue, for fear I would only intensify existing prejudices and stereotypes. I chose instead to include my recommendations for women within my discussion of more general business concerns.

I learned, however, that the subject of women doing business with

Japan was a key one not only for individuals but for organizations, and I started to approach it in a more focused and systematic manner. Japanese male acquaintances also came to me for advice on how to correct their own bad reputations and for concrete guidelines on how they could work better with Western women. Both of these are real concerns for male corporate Japan for two reasons: (1) Japan has a serious labor shortage and must now hire educated Japanese women for positions previously held only by men, and (2) Japan is now finding that when conducting business internationally, women are at every level of the business transactions.

Until recently, Japanese men have had no experience working with women. But the traditional picture of a workplace with few or no women is changing so rapidly that many Japanese men have been caught unprepared. Japan today imports workers from other countries to fill its menial jobs. But for its educated workforce the country is increasingly turning to its own women. Forty percent of the Japanese workforce, including part-timers, is now female. Yet the attrition rate for college-educated women is forty-five percent. Where do all these women go? Given the societal pressures to quit work and start a home and family, many do just that, creating a constantly changing workforce that is underutilized and certainly not as productive as it could be. Another significant portion of these educated women go abroad or to foreign companies for opportunities not yet available to them at home.

Japan is acutely aware that it must find ways to attract the female worker, not only by minimizing the attrition rate of those in administrative positions, but also by keeping the college-educated female interested in a professional career. With passage of the Equal Opportunity Law in 1986, Japanese companies have opened the door to career women. The government has also issued directives advising companies to hire more women and has compiled videos on effective ways to manage a female worker. But the fact of maternity and the duties of motherhood continue to be cited as reasons why women cannot be managerial track employees. A more substantial effort at easing women into managerial levels is a recently passed bill that allows a year of maternity leave and, in most cases, does away with the requirement that all career-track employees must sign an agreement that they will allow themselves to be transferred to any site dictated by the needs of the company.

How earnestly Japanese companies will pursue these new policies is yet to be seen. And what impact foreign companies with females in senior executive positions will have is a story still in the making. Professional women, however few, do exist in Japan, and the road they have carved out thus far is an important one.

Armed with this as background, Tracey and I pooled our experiences in the creation of this book. We hope it serves you well in your business interactions with Japan (and with Japanese men).

By Tracey Wilen

FOR MY MOTHER—THE DOCTOR

As a successful female professional, you have not only been my role model but the model for many aspiring professional women. You were successful in a time when it was not fashionable for women to excel in their careers. You persevered to meet your goals of career, family, and a successful marriage, and you took the time to share your strength with me. I am exhausted when I think of how much time you have spent with me to help me achieve my own goals. You have encouraged me to move ahead when I thought I couldn't, or when people said it wasn't possible. Thanks for telling me I could be whatever I wanted to be. You broadened my life by exposing me to the value of education and travel. I am thrilled that I have been able to learn your greatest talents: questioning and listening. They have helped me write this book and become who I am. I have always watched you in awe. I have always been so proud of you. I hope you will be proud of me and enjoy the results of this work. Thank you for still always being there for me, for listening, for editing (!), and for just being mom.

Every business today is affected by the international marketplace, from the small neighborhood grocery that imports fruit from South America to the automobile factory in Ohio that brings in steel and engines from Asia. Knowing how to do business in countries other than our own is therefore critical to economic survival; it is also challenging, since the world is very large and business and social practices vary from culture to culture.

My first global business experience took place over a decade ago, and about five years ago I started working with Japan. Japan was very different from what my previous experience had led me to expect. I had had no warning or training about how to establish good working relationships with the Japanese. So I read lots of books. I drove my friends, family, and colleagues crazy as I looked for the magic golden rules of succeeding in business with the Japanese. I took courses, and even redirected my graduate business courses to a concentration on Japanese business.

What emerged from my studies was the understanding that extrapolating from one's own culture to another is a big mistake. You can't assume that everyone in business acts, thinks, or organizes the same as you do, or has the same priorities. Nor can you assume that people within a culture are all identical, although their physical features and basic value systems may make them appear that way. Business decisions always need to be looked at on their individual merits, but within the cultural context in which they occur. The best international businesspeople are those intuitive enough to navigate around these cultural differences by learning how to work within them. Coming to understand your foreign business partners is not easy. It takes time, a broad perspective, and the willingness to understand.

In the case of Japan, all Western businesspeople need to be aware of the many profound differences between Japanese and Western cultures to avoid misunderstandings. But it is particularly important that Western businesswomen be aware of these differences, since they can create invisible barriers to their credibility and effectiveness when working with Japanese men.

Japanese men are just about the only people in authority most Western businesswomen will ever meet in Japan, since women typically do not hold high positions in Japanese firms. Japanese men are not accustomed to women conducting business on their own, and they view women as less capable of handling business problems and in need of more supervision and direction than male staff. Working with women in positions of authority makes Japanese men exceedingly uncomfortable. Most Japanese men would say that "The man is on call for the company and the woman on call for the family." This inability of most Japanese men to even imagine a female functioning in the business world places Western businesswomen at an immediate disadvantage in Japan.

Women seeking to establish a toehold where they were never welcome before benefit from having a mentor. In the business environment, mentoring is an invaluable tool for women wishing to move up the ranks. As the sole woman in a group of businessmen traveling to Japan, I remember begin treated differently from my male colleagues. I was something of a spectacle to the Japanese men our group visited. They asked questions of me first as a professional and then as a single woman, and this made me very uneasy. I tried adjusting my business style in an effort to blend in. I found myself reaching for books, learning materials, and other women to see if everything I was feeling was normal. Men can be terrific support systems. But they are not women, and they do not face what many of us do. So my company colleagues were of little help.

Chris and I met about two years ago. As a student in her seminars on doing business with Japan I recall sharing with her some of my frustrations and successes. She was the first woman I found who could really identify with my experiences with the Japanese. We found ourselves chatting over lunch on the lack of good Japan materials available for women. We spontaneously came to the same conclusion that we were both in perfect positions to gather advice into a guidebook that would fill that need—a book for women by women. Chris in her seminars and I through my frequent visits to Japan often came into contact with businesswomen working with the Japanese. Many of these women were successful, yet each one had had to find her own way. Why not let their insights and experiences—and their mistakes—guide the rest of us?

That's what we hope has come about in this book. In all Chris and I interviewed over two hundred women in fields as diverse as high technology, fashion, retailing, law, travel, entertainment, advertising, marketing, and industrial sales. All these women were ready and willing to serve as mentors to the rest of us. We can't bring you these women in person (and we cannot identify them either, for obvious reasons), but we have been able to bring you some of their experiences in their own words. We hope you will learn from what they have to say, and in turn that you will share with other women your own advice and your successes. We would also recommend that men read this book too, so they can better support their female colleagues and learn about an aspect of Japanese business culture that they might otherwise be blithely unaware of.

One Final Note

It is not our purpose to tell the Japanese how to live their lives or what to believe. However, just as American corporations insist that their foreign partners do not engage in graft, exploit their workers, or support dictatorial governments that are hostile to fundamental human rights, we feel it is perfectly legitimate to insist that Japanese companies doing business globally adhere to fair and nonsexist practices, both at home and abroad.

The resistance to change in Japan may be simply that and nothing more. As time passes, many of Japan's old, inhibiting customs and beliefs will surely fade away. Even at this writing, the status of women in Japan is changing rapidly, just as more and more Western women are traveling to Japan and doing business with the Japanese. As a result, Japanese men are gradually becoming accustomed to the idea that a woman can have negotiating and decision-making power. But that is no excuse for women to simply wait and hope for the best. If women in Japan and women doing business with Japan want change, they must—as women have so often done in the past—force the issue and refuse to back down.

Throughout, you will see the term "OL" or "office lady." This is what the Japanese call female officeworkers that hold low-level administrative positions. We've kept the usage, but only in a specifically Japanese context to illustrate the Japanese way of viewing and using these working women.

Our thanks to the many women and men who contributed to the making of this book. Our thanks to you for reading it. We hope it helps make your lives a little easier and a lot more profitable.

PART 1

HANDBOOK

Establishing Your Authority

"Parrot time" is my group's name for what we women experience when one of us answers a question directed to our team and no one on the Japanese side, including the questioner, listens or even looks at us. Then, when one of our male colleagues repeats exactly what we just said, the Japanese faces all light up in instant comprehension. This game can go on indefinitely, and is just as uncomfortable for our male colleagues who are forced to parrot what we've said. We have a strategy for this. When parroting threatens, a male colleague defers by saying, "Carol is the authority on that. She's the one who should answer your question" or "Carol knows more about that subject than I do." This works very well. (Boise, Idaho)

The first thing you have to establish in any business meeting is your authority. To say you have "authority" means you speak with the full support of your company behind you. Authority flows from legitimacy. In public life, legitimacy is conferred by the voters. In corporate life—at least among men—legitimacy flows from one's position or rank.

It is odd that in Japan, a nation known for its rigid observance of hierarchy, women in legitimate positions of power in business are constantly having their authority questioned. This is not the case in traditionally "female" arts in Japan like tea or flower arranging, so it must be the case that problems arise in business because the woman there is considered a fish out of water—out of her league and out of her depth. That you as a woman might be more competent, powerful, and intelligent than everyone else in the Tokyo meeting room has nothing to do with it—you're an anomaly from the get-go, and *that's* the first obstacle to overcome.

Most Japanese businessmen are well aware that, when dealing in the global market, they will be working with men and women at all levels of authority. They also know that such dealings are not one-shot deals, that they must continue learning how to work within very diverse cultural contexts. Despite the good intentions of these gentlemen, however, they may not know how to behave properly. Perfectly reasonable questions for them might be "Is it OK to smile at a woman at a business meeting?" "How much courtesy will be considered sexist?" "Should I step aside and let her enter the elevator before I do?" "Do I stand up when she enters the room?" "Will she feel that I am not respecting her position if I treat her like a lady?" And sometimes the fear of making a mistake may unwittingly lead them to doing things that dilute your authority just the same.

And of course you will meet the men who aren't so thoughtful and are really out to undermine you. In Japan, remember to look for the small, whittling attitudes—these are more subtle and damaging than the direct attack, which would be a great breach of Japanese protocol. It is the small gestures that can lead to wrong first impressions, mistrust, and confrontations. These may also serve as keys to the greater, underlying prejudices in the corporate culture. When the top-ranking member of a Japanese team is allowed to make sexist remarks without challenge, there is no reason to expect his subordinates to change their thinking either.

You should try to determine whether the Japanese attitude is an attempt to question or undermine your authority—or just an insensitive, sexist remark based on unfamiliarity and ignorance. An accurate assessment at this stage will help you pick an effective course of action to prevent more complex problems later. In every case, personal confidence is the key to establishing your authority—confidence in the way you walk, sit, stand, dress, respond, and speak. Each of your mannerisms is a vehicle for defining and asserting your authority.

Jn Their Own Words

POWER SEATING

When I held my first meeting with the Japanese, I knew I had to establish my credibility immediately. I asked my team members to enter the room first, introduce themselves, and be seated. I told them not to start the meeting until I joined them and to leave the center seat at the negotiating table open for me. Better than any verbal introduction or business card, these very visible actions clearly established my position and authority. Equally important, they showed the Japanese that our negotiating team was unified and organized. (New York City, New York)

THE JOKE ABOUT MY TITLE

During a major presentation, an articulate Japanese man nitpicked at almost every sentence of mine with mostly irrelevant questions. He hemmed and hawed at each of my answers, and repeatedly asked me to verify the opinions of my male colleagues. Such interruptions can throw even the quickest presenter off, and if this happens to you you should politely ask that all questions be reserved until the end of the meeting.

But problems like this one usually start even before the presentation begins, for example when your business card is presented and your position is not fully understood or appreciated by the Japanese receiver. An awkward joke about my title should have clued me in to my problem listener's confusion about the power a female can hold in Western society and my own role at the meeting. At that time I ignored his "joke," thinking the humor was probably lost in translation. This was a mistake. If you realize that your authority is being undermined by jokes or incessant interruptions, stop the chitchat and the business and clarify your position. Do this immediately by going over your credentials as politely and diplomatically as possible. Say something like "Yes, I am in charge of this project. I'm very sorry you were not advised in advance."

Then, during informal discussions, sprinkle your conversation with comments about your credentials and experience. The length of time at your firm, your alma mater, and the degrees you hold are all good things to have the Japanese know.

After a quick but polite "reprimand," it would take a bold individual to keep up the insults. I say bold because it would be the rare Japanese who could make such interruptions when it is clear they are taken as insults to you and your company. (Boston, Massachusetts)

TO SERVE TEA OR NOT TO SERVE TEA

A team of Japanese engineers was visiting us in the U.S. I was a new member on our team and would be in charge of the Japanese group on this project. On the first day of their visit I had to arrive after our meeting with them had already begun. Not wanting to disrupt things, I did not initially offer my business card. A staff member simply introduced me by name but without my title. During the meeting, one of the Japanese team members asked if I would get him some tea. I realized that he had mistaken me for a secretary. I didn't want to embarrass him, but I also realized that getting him his tea would be more embarrassing in the long-run—not to mention undermining my position. So I suggested to the entire group that we take a tea break, and I then asked one of my staff to set up refreshments. Now we make sure that positions for late entrants or silent observers are clearly established to avoid misinterpretations of roles and responsibilities. We also make sure that observers are allowed to present their business cards at the first opportunity. (Santa Clara, California)

APOLOGY WITH SWEAT

Our Japanese supplier was having a quality problem on our product line. It was affecting our revenue, and the Japanese had come to apologize to our firm. The senior executive made a formal apology and sat down. Then the lead engineer got up and spoke for forty-five minutes. He presented the recovery plan in great detail. He was nervous, having difficulty speaking, and sweating buckets. It was quite a sight. When he finally finished, he concluded by saying, "I am very sorry. Please accept my apology."

I, the highest ranking individual, then said, "We accept your apology. Thank you very much for your presentation."

But instead of showing relief, he looked like he was ready to kill himself. Absolution from a woman obviously wasn't enough for him. We had had a relationship with this vendor for a number of years, yet it was clear he refused to acknowledge my position. He thought we weren't satisfied with his explanation and did not really accept his apology. It was pure sexism. As uncomfortable as it was for him, and since no one on my team caught on that he was waiting for them to apologize too, I again said that I appreciated his explanation and apology. Then I let him sit down and continue to sweat it out for a bit longer. (Boise, Idaho)

THE GOPHER

As the last one to go into the meeting room I seated myself in the chair nearest the door. During the meeting, one of my male colleagues asked me to go photocopy a document since (he said later) I was in a convenient location. I did it, but it was hard for me to recover my credibility with the Japanese team. It looked like I was his secretary or his assistant, when in fact I was neither.

Women, you should voice your credibility concerns to your male team members (who may otherwise take advantage of your gender as a way to boost themselves). Men may also not realize what a difficult position they can put women in by so seemingly trivial a request. Tell men about authority and Japanese realities, and explain how the whole team suffers if your authority is undermined. Be proactive within your own group. For example, invite a secretary to the meeting to take care of the administrative or serving tasks as they arise. (San Jose, California)

FINESSE IT

Tom, my male colleague, and I have a female manager, Jane. We three realized that Tom, despite introductions to the contrary, might be perceived by the Japanese as the decision maker on our team. To avoid this possibility, we came up with the following plan. Jane, our manager, would make the introductory speech at the meeting, take the listener seat, and observe the meetings. I would take the center seat and be the speaker and analyzer of the negotiations. I would defer to Jane for important decisions and motion for her approval on agreements as they came up. During the meeting, Tom would sit by the door, make copies of all documents, assist the caterer, and take phone messages—as well as present his own part of the package. So although Tom would look after all the administrative duties, he would also be a key player. The final decisions, however, would always be made by Jane.

By positioning ourselves in this way we made the most of each of our roles. Sometimes a little finessing is necessary to establish the working relationship with the Japanese. We found that a little less rigidity in our roles was possible after the third or fourth meeting. (Austin, Texas)

THE OUTBURST

I was making a presentation in Tokyo to a very reserved all-Japanese audience. I was desperately trying to add life to the session by being friendly and casual. I wanted visual feedback, but nothing was working. As a last resort, as I often do in the U.S., I tossed aside my written text and made a joke involving a harmless English expletive. I waited for the chuckles—for an eternity. The audience sat in silence. Nobody moved a muscle. The joke was misunderstood.

Humor is cross cultural, but jokes are not. My joke had been misinterpreted, and once I realized it I immediately became more formal and focused on the subject matter. It worked, and I'll never make that mistake again. When you make presentations to the Japanese keep to the facts—no matter how boring they may be. (Penang, Malaysia)

FUNNY FACES

My first presentation to the Japanese was as a panelist. During my speech I could not help noticing a senior Japanese executive in the audience. The man was, for all the world, just sitting there making faces at me! He squinted, frowned, wrinkled his nose, and pursed his lips. It was a sight to behold—nothing I was prepared for—and I couldn't decide if I was more insulted, outraged, or mortified. I finished my talk and then related the experience to a friend who knew the senior executive quite well. I wondered aloud if I should confront the situation. He offered to take it up with him on my behalf.

Well, an apology arrived immediately. The man was unaware of what he had been doing. He had unconsciously been caught up in mimicking my facial expressions. Like many Japanese males, he was not used to seeing women so animated. So now I tone down the emotions and gestures during my presentations. (Milpitas, California)

EXPERTS BEWARE

When you speak Japanese or are perceived by your company as a "Japan expert," you have to prepare your management for the reactions you may get from the Japanese. Being bilingual and having lived in Japan for twenty years, I work exclusively with my company's Japanese clients and get a great deal of information from them that others cannot. Sometimes, though, I can make my clients uncomfortable by speaking fluent Japanese and understanding a great deal more about their way of doing business than the Westerners they are used to. The kinds of reactions I get run the gamut from expressions of shock that I know how to use chopsticks to remarks such as "Her Japanese isn't all that good" (even though it is native).

I explain these reactions to my CEO, who is from Texas, by asking him to imagine how he would react to a kimono-clad Japanese businessman who greets him in Tokyo by leaning back in his chair, kicking off his sandals, lighting up a Havana, and speaking English with a perfect Texas drawl.

Contemplate the options you have as a native or fluent speaker of Japanese. Use your Japanese if you think it will help overcome cultural barriers and tighten your relationship. Hold off on it for a while if you think it might be taken as an insult by the other side (as if to say their English isn't good enough, for example). And avoid it altogether if it means you will be used by either company as an interpreter during meetings. (New Haven, Connecticut)

Dos and Don'ts

BEFORE YOU GO

❏ Always plan to work and travel with a team.

❑ Decide who are the team members and what areas of expertise they will represent at the meeting.

❑ Decide who will conduct the meeting as the speaker, and who will observe.

❑ Plan out the seating for your team. Put your spokesperson in the center seat. Place your observer and most senior person in the seat farthest from the door.

❑ If your role is that of the observer, don't plan to control the meeting. Listening is construed as authoritative by the Japanese.

❑ If you are the speaker, instruct your colleagues to direct questions to you and defer to you as needed.

❑ If you are the chairwoman, plan an introduction speech and some closing remarks. Advise your team not to debate with you or with each other during the meetings.

❑ Prepare a strategy for your visit: What is the purpose, what are your alternatives, when do you need your answers, what do you plan to resolve at the meetings?

❑ Anticipate and have answers for any questions that may arise during your visit.

❑ Have a plan of action you will take if a conflict arises. It may be to excuse the group from the room, or to drop the subject and discuss it later among yourselves.

❑ Decide what data need to be collected before you go.

❑ Prepare copies of all required documents for everyone on both sides who will be attending the meeting.

❑ Prepare plenty of business cards for your entire team, as there will be many occasions where they are required.

❑ Always have your card translated into Japanese on one side. This shows courtesy and also that you are not a last-minute replacement on your team. Failing to have Japanese on your card can seriously undermine your authority.

❏ Don't use titles like Specialist or Strategic on your business cards. These are too vague to most Japanese. As a women, you should have a strong title like Senior Manager or Director. If you need to change your title to something more meaningful so your Japanese counterparts understand your importance, then do so. Many women keep a separate box of business cards for Japanese business sessions.

❏ If this is your first meeting with Japanese colleagues, have an introductory fax or letter sent in advance. This letter should come from someone higher than yourself in the firm and preferably someone who personally knows the head of the Japanese team with whom you will be meeting.

❏ The letter of introduction should introduce the members of the team, their responsibilities, and their titles. It should introduce you as the chairwoman or chief negotiator if that is your role.

❏ If you will be conducting the meeting, also send a fax or letter in advance that outlines the agenda and the topics you would like to cover.

❏ If you have a special request for data you would like to have presented at the meeting, outline this in advance via fax or letter. The Japanese like to be very prepared and to present their findings at business meetings.

WHEN YOU ARE THERE

❏ Advise your hosts of your travel arrangements and transportation.

❏ Because you are a woman, your hosts may feel obligated to meet you at the airport and take care of you. If you do not want to accept this courtesy let your hosts know, since otherwise they may be waiting for you at the airport when you arrive.

❏ If you are the chairwoman and lead person, clearly introduce yourself as the principal contact person for your hosts.

❑   As the leader of your group, you may be invited to meet with your go-between or Japan contact the night before the meeting. Your host may simply want to touch base and get the relationship going over a drink or dinner in the hotel. He will become your interface throughout your stay. Use this time to review the meeting agenda and request any changes. You might also want to introduce your team so you all have a familiar face the next day.

❑   If you have subsidiary associates coming in from other parts of Japan, initiate a pre-meeting the morning of your visit in your hotel over breakfast. This may be the first time you meet with them and it is wise to know each other upon arriving at your hosts' firm.

❑   Always arrive together as a group.

❑   When you arrive, have your subsidiary associate introduce your team, yourself first, to the receptionist. If you have no associate, you take the initiative.

❑   Someone will come out to greet you. Have your business cards ready for introductions. (Place them in your jacket pocket or some other place that is easy to reach.)

❑   Enter the room first, before your team, to show that you are the leader of the group. You should be the first one on your team to present your business card. Always present it to the highest ranking member of the Japanese team first.

❑   Present and accept the Japanese cards with both hands. Accepting with one hand is OK, but two hands is more courteous. State your own name and title as you present your card. Make sure your title and position is understood.

❑   Graciously accept the Japanese card with as much formality as you can muster. You are not likely to overdo it.

❑   Make sure your interpreter is at your side to translate anything in the greetings for both sides. Keep the interpreter nearby as your assistant throughout the meeting.

❏ Seating is extremely important in Japanese business. Allow your hosts to seat you. Most likely you will be placed in the middle of the side of the table farthest from the door, since this is the place of honor. Your hosts will align themselves across from you according to rank or title. The ends of the table will be left open. See "Business Seating Charts" at the back of this book.

❏ Have your counterparts address and refer to you by your last name instead of your first name. This is more in keeping with the formality necessary for first meetings and will help establish your authority. Typically, Japanese address women by their first names and men by their last names.

❏ Use the first meeting as a chance to get acquainted. Even in business, Japanese will often overlook the bottom line for people with whom they can feel comfortable in a long-term relationship.

❏ Spend the first part of the meeting asking your counterparts questions about their company, their jobs, and their product lines. Allow them to ask you questions as well.

❏ "Office ladies" will go in and out of the room carrying tea and drinks. They will not be introduced and you are not to introduce yourself or team members to them. Do not interfere with their tasks or offer to help out.

BEFORE THEY VISIT YOU

❏ Initiate a draft agenda by fax or letter for the meeting. Ask if there are special subjects the other side wants to discuss.

❏ Ask for a list of the attendees and their titles in advance. Try to choose appropriate counterparts in rank and title from your firm to attend the meeting. Be sure to ask if any people other than the listed attendees will be at the meeting; often the Japanese send junior people in training to take notes and observe but take not role in the negotiations.

❏ Assemble your team and decide on roles. Prepare presentation materials and documentation for all attendees on each side.

❑ Choose a room with enough seating for the entire group. Use a rectangular meeting table.

❑ Have audio/visual equipment ready in case your counterparts bring presentations for the meeting.

❑ Plan your agenda with time for breaks and meals.

❑ Assign an individual to handle all administrative duties during the meeting. Do not do this yourself.

❑ Arrange a caterer or office staff member to serve during breaks. Do not serve yourself.

❑ If you are in a negotiation session, arrange to have an extra room available for private group discussions by either side.

❑ Advise your team in advance that you will lead them out of the room if you sense prolonged tension (which may indeed occur if you are in a negotiation session).

❑ Plan to host a welcome dinner. Request that your entire team attend the dinner as a courtesy.

WHEN THEY ARE HERE

❑ You may wish to arrange transportation for your guests. Try to have someone in your office greet your guests at their hotels and usher them to their offices.

❑ Always greet your guests as a team. Initiate the business card exchange as soon as your guests have arrived.

❑ If you are the chairwoman, take the lead in the introductions and business card exchange. You should also be the one to lead your guests and your team into the meeting room. (Some women prefer to have their guests greeted, ushered, and seated in the room by their assistants before coming into the room themselves.)

❑ Invite your guests to be seated on the far side of the room (the side away from the door). You and your team should wait until the Japanese are seated before sitting down yourselves.

❏   If you are chairing the meeting, seat yourself in the center on your side of the table. If you are observing, sit at the chair farthest from the door on your side (so no one thinks you're there to run errands).

❏   If you are observing as the highest ranking person at the meeting, you should be the one to give the opening and closing remarks.

❏   If you are chairing the meeting, it is still a good idea that you deliver the opening and closing remarks. Do not overlook any opportunity to add to your credibility and authority up front.

❏   Always begin your opening remarks by thanking your guests for traveling such a great distance to visit you. This is appropriate even if your guests are the ones who are seeking business from you.

❏   Closing remarks should address partnering if appropriate or "mutual prosperity."

❏   If the meeting is a presentation, invite your guests to go first. Help them with all the furnishings and equipment.

❏   Have refreshments replenished periodically during the meeting by staff. Don't help out.

GENERAL MEETING PROTOCOL

❏   If you are outranked by a female manager on your team, you will both need to establish your credibility and should play your respective roles.

❏   If you are one of two or more women at a meeting, have your male colleagues assist you by taking on lesser, administrative roles. This will add to your credibility. The men do not need to establish theirs as much.

❏   Do not fall into the pattern of one woman on your team serving the other. Have a male serve you both.

❏ Never take the seat closest to the door, or you may be mistaken for administrative help.

❏ When there is a break for everyone to go out of the room for a stretch, you may find that someone from the other side will approach you for a quiet, off-line discussion. Woman are viewed as mediators and you may find that you have been selected to break the tension. You may also wish to propose yourself as a mediator, in which case you can be the one to start up a discreet discussion during the break.

❏ Keep a whiteboard in the room. Many times members of either side will wish to use a sketch or flow chart to help explain a point.

❏ If it is a negotiation, assign someone to keep notes of all agreements made during the meeting. Then review all agreements before your guests leave. Have the notes distributed later if you can.

❏ Keep a calculator with you. A women is perceived as stronger when she is adept with numbers.

❏ Don't use direct eye contact all the time. Practice glancing away during a discussion. Japanese do not use direct eye contact unless they are extremely westernized. It is considered rude.

❏ Don't be unapproachable or overly friendly from the start. Be pleasantly polite.

❏ Don't be confrontational with the Japanese. Use questions to draw out their point of view.

❏ Don't get flustered by periods of silence. Japanese typically use silence either to contemplate or to express disagreement. Pay attention to how the silence is used and learn to use it yourself. Silence, if used judiciously, is a powerful tool.

❏ Use a strong, nonemotional voice when you are speaking.

❏ Minimize your facial expressions, since women are stereotyped as being too emotional. Make particularly sure you do not use the deferential posture or high voice commonly adopted by Japanese women in formal situations.

❑ Speak slowly and with all proper articles. It is not OK to take out the "a" and the "the" from your speech. Japanese will know you are talking this way and will be insulted. (This is an easy speech pattern to fall into, since non-native speakers will often drop the articles in their speech to you.)

❑ Don't increase your volume when speaking. The Japanese can hear and understand you. (But be aware that speaking louder is a natural tendency when talking to people who don't speak your language well.)

❑ Don't use slang or incomplete sentences. Don't use long-winded, complex sentences. This can be very confusing, and you may have people nodding out of courtesy when they really don't understand.

❑ Don't use big words. Why use "feasible" when "possible" is just as good, or "gargantuan" when "big" will do and be more easily understood?

❑ Language experts: Don't use your skill as an interpreter at the meeting. If an interpreter is needed the other side will bring one, and you may desire to have another interpreter of your own. Use your language skill for the more informal channels of communication, but not during formal meetings, presentations, or negotiations. However, using Japanese briefly for opening and closing remarks will be considered very gracious.

When You Are the Senior Executive

I was at home watching a live television interview of a woman who was a senior executive of a U.S.-based multinational computer company. A reporter turned to her and asked, "Did you get your present position by ability or by sleeping around?" (Tokyo, Japan)

While the Japanese may have trouble dealing with you as a woman in business, your title and rank if you are a CEO or senior vice-president do carry some hierarchical significance. At the very least they make it clear you will *not* be making photocopies for your team and that ultimately you are the decision maker. Your position also gives you the ability to marshal the forces of your company to make your legitimacy plainly visible in ways that are both meaningful and unambiguous. And that's exactly what you should do.

A woman in a senior management position needs to "do it right the first time." In Japan, nothing lasts like a first impression.

Look the part—dress should be conservative in style and color with little or no accessories (see the chapter "What to Wear").

Act the part—your self-presentation should be reserved, decorous, formally friendly, never light-hearted or jovial.

Speak the part—your communication style should be concise, dignified, and definitive, in a word, authoritative. As a senior executive of high visibility, you epitomize your company's integrity in a way a less prominent member does not.

So "position" yourself right from the start and avoid a lot of headaches. The complexities of intercultural communication and prejudice being what they are, failure at the starting line will stall negotiations and render you ineffective as a future decision maker in Japan. Damage control will only make things worse.

But what if the slight has already been made? What should that senior executive on television have done?

She should *not* have gotten angry because, in Japanese eyes, that would be seen as a lack of dignity and self-discipline, something a person of her rank and authority must show at all times. She should *not* have ignored the question, in hopes that, by staying aloof, the problem would go away. In fact, the situation would most likely have gotten worse and her silence would have been mistaken for a confirmation of the implied accusation. And, under no circumstances should she have countered with a joke: "Sleeping around? Oh, definitely, sleeping, oh let me see, around four or five hours a night. That's my secret!" Making light of this situation is the worst thing she could have done.

The *correct* response in such a situation, public and private, is always the kind of polite, but firm and authoritative, remark that puts the woman in a morally and intellectually superior position to her potential victimizer, thus shaming him from future actions of the same kind. We suggest: "Of course by ability. And as you might know, your question is unacceptable." Then she should completely ignore the individual who tried to insult her.

Jn Their Own Words

HE WOULDN'T SHAKE MY HAND

The senior Japanese man shook everybody's hand but mine.

This was in Japan, where our senior executives and those of the Japanese company were meeting to discuss "future directions of cooperation and interest." During the formal introductions, the Japanese team went right down the receiving line, shaking hands and exchanging greetings with each of my colleagues. I, the only woman on our board, received a quick and dismissive glance.

Since this was a very conservative Japanese company that had not done a great deal of international business, I chose not to react to this slight. Intercultural issues and protocol can be very complex. A handshake can be viewed as sexual and nonbusinesslike from a woman. A quick bow or "nod" might be a sufficient greeting in that case. On trips to Japan now, I feel more comfortable if I initiate the introduction with a handshake.

I also restrain my naturally assertive communication style and act a bit formal and polite. I've found this to be an effective tool for asserting power, rather than just trying to push my way through. But I advise women to ease into this mode, and pay attention to how you are being perceived by the Japanese. (Santa Clara, California)

YES, SHE IS THE DIRECTOR

Most of my staff is stationed around the world. As director of a large firm, I spend most of my time traveling alone. My staff manager in Japan is Japanese. He schedules all my meetings and appointments there. I would describe our relationship as very good.

On occasion, I ask my manager to arrange visits to our Japanese clients. My last visit was to a firm outside Tokyo proper—my first excursion away from the metropolitan mainstream of Japanese business. This particular firm was very traditional compared with the big-city types I was familiar with. Very formal.

To my surprise, my staff manager also behaved quite differently toward me on this visit. His introductions were unusually long and exquisitely formal. He'd defer to me in almost every aspect of Japanese etiquette, emphasizing over and over again that I was a director in the U.S. firm. I sensed a high degree of discomfort at my visit among the men in the Japanese company. Some of them would not rise to shake hands with me, and I got next to no eye contact.

My manager was clearly anxious about presenting a woman as his company's executive. Anticipating rejection, he had been taking steps to save face for me. I appreciated his intuitiveness and reacted as if nothing was out of the ordinary, in calculated ignorance of the palpable tension on both sides. While there are differences between Japanese companies, home and abroad, it is best to let nationals who understand the culture establish your authority. And always, always err on the side of formality and personal restraint. (San Francisco, California)

A WOMAN CHANGED THE PRICE?!

My first contact with our Japanese distributor was three years ago by fax, right after I had replaced a man in my position. The Japanese did not realize that they were now doing business with a woman since we only communicated by fax. During my first few months on the job, I restructured both the pricing and product line of our company—raising our prices quite a bit. This was accepted until the Japanese realized that it was a woman who was responsible for the price increases. They contacted the CEO of my company to complain. Do you realize you have a woman who is setting the pricing? they were saying, expecting that the CEO would immediately put a stop to that nonsense. But the boss stood behind me. The point here is that you should always make sure you have the support of your management and that they will support your decision if it is questioned. (Memphis, Tennessee)

X-RATED

I was making a major address at an international conference in Japan, and as a result I had attendants with me from the time I got off the plane. Every night was a dinner or a tea ceremony, and all the elegant protocol was observed meticulously. One night, the planned festivities included a visit to a posh Japanese club. Many of the people who attended brought their spouses, so there was a fair mix of men and women. What to my surprise when the X-rated dancers came out, stripping and grinding on the runway. I couldn't believe this had been included for people at this prestigious conference. Every woman in the audience must have felt the same embarrassment. If a client of mine had taken me to such a place I would have insisted on leaving, but here it would have had too much of a negative impact on the conference had I walked out the door. I know every woman in the place would have followed me too. I decided that this was not the place to take a stance on sexism. (Tokyo, Japan)

DIRECT OR INDIRECT?

I am a director of my company's home office in the U.S. My problems were with the Japanese manager of our Tokyo subsidiary. The guy absolutely refused to mail or fax any important documents to me directly. Anything he thought important would be sent to my boss, a man. Major delays, major aggravation.

I had the usual and obvious choice in such a situation. I could take the direct approach by confronting him and his boss with the consequences of his actions, demand an explanation for such irresponsibility, and insist that it never happen again. Or I could take the indirect approach in order to help him "save face." I chose the second approach. I wrote him a letter in which, while not referring to any of his previous actions, I requested that he please send all important communications to me directly. I repeatedly emphasized the time-sensitive nature of the information and the sorts of problems that could arise from even the shortest delays in remittance. I sent the letter to him but made sure he noted that copies were also being sent to his boss and mine.

That solved my problem.

You have to assess the nature of the problem and whether the best solution involves direct or indirect action. Japanese men in general respond very well to indirect corrective actions like mine, where I copied upper management on my letter.

There will be times, however, when the direct approach is best, and I have a story illustrating that too. My counterpart on the West Coast and I are women in charge of shipping our company's products worldwide. From the very first we encountered problems working with our Japanese clients. For example our calls were not returned but our male colleagues' were. Letters intended for us were addressed to male employees at our firm. Business discussions that we were chairing weren't attended.

We decided to confront the Japanese at one of our meetings. "We have no problem with women," they said. "Then why," I countered, "don't you, Mr. Yamada, return my calls?" No response. I tried again. "Why do you always correspond only with our vice president, who has nothing to do with our own transactions? Is it just because he is a man?" After some hemming and hawing, the answer, again predictably, was: "We have no problem with women."

We finally had to do what we'd hoped to avoid. "It appears to us," I said, "that you do have a problem working with women. And since you don't seem willing to address it, we regretfully have to inform you that our company will accept outside bids at the conclusion of the present contract."

I felt the situation here was serious enough to use a direct approach with this firm. Considering how their attitude was impacting our business, it did not make sense to politely maneuver around the problem. As a footnote, I should note that three months later the Japanese company lost five million dollars of incremental business and appointed a foreign woman as project coordinator to deal with us. We don't yet know how this new arrangement will work, but we take it as an attempt on the Japanese side to address the problem and are now accepting bids from them again. (Boston, Massachusetts)

DON'T GET HONORED OR FORMALIZED TO DEATH

I was promoted by my firm as director of our Japan subsidiary, a position a woman, of course, had never held before. Now that I look back at it, there was a great deal of maneuvering to undermine my effectiveness. You might say I was killed with kindness. Honored to death.

First I was asked by the subsidiary to delay my arrival to Japan until they could create an appropriate office for me. I complied. When I arrived I noted that I was put in a nice roomy office, away from everyone and out of the mainstream of information flow. I was also given an elaborate welcoming party and treated with great formality and courtesy. I couldn't get anyone to really talk to me.

I then had to work extra hard to become effective. Here are a couple things I did:

• I moved my desk out of the formal office, and into the common area with the rest of the staff, just like all the other Japanese executives.

• I established myself as director by making the business decisions that needed to be made.

• I spent the first three months concentrating on the personal connections so that my decisions could be more easily implemented.

Formality, although very nice and flattering, is a barrier if it lasts too long. Japanese formal communication, if kept too formal too long, is a means of keeping you at a distance and ultimately of not communicating with you at all. (Tokyo, Japan)

BEING A BURDEN IS GOOD

This happened in New York. Our major Japanese client was hosting us at an elaborate dinner. There were fifty or more VIPs.

I wasn't feeling well and needed to bow out early. I waited until the dinner was over and the first round of toasts was exchanged. Then, after informing my superior, I quietly exited. All was well until, waiting for my coat and a cab, I was told by the concierge not to leave yet. Ten minutes later, the president of the Japanese company rushed up to express his concern for my health, insisting in no uncertain terms that his personal limousine take me to my hotel—he himself would take a cab. After much hemming and hawing, I finally had to accept his gracious offer of assistance.

Here is a quick lesson in Japanese hospitality: Accept, and accept graciously, offers of help no matter how much trouble they may appear to cause your hosts. Both the offer and your acceptance are important parts of the business relationship, and both are an attempt to make a connection, forge a personal bond, that will last far beyond the immediate occasion. Too many times in the past I refused those little acts of charity—"Let me hail you a taxi," "Let me copy that for you," etc.—because I didn't want to be a burden to my Japanese hosts and because I assumed that they expected my refusal.

But in many areas of Japanese social life and etiquette, there is the idea "I'll let you be a burden to me, if you'll let me be a burden to you—let's be burdens to each other." Your acceptance of such personal overtures indicates your willingness to commit to the social intimacy and mutual trust that are essential to any successful business relationship with the Japanese, whether you're in New York or Tokyo.

So be a burden. Being a burden can be a good thing. (New York City, New York)

Dos and Don'ts

❑   Be polite, calm, restrained. These are qualities attributed in Japan to people with real authority.

❑ Be formal but not unfriendly.

❑ As a woman you must be careful of what you say, how you act, and how you appear. You will stand out, and you will make a more lasting visual impression than a male executive. Any error you make will be multiplied in magnitude. Anything noteworthy you do will likewise be remembered.

❑ Let others help establish your authority through third-party communication at the time you are preparing for your trip. A local office staff member is a good person to help establish your status.

❑ Travel with staff whose lower ranking can be used to set off your higher position.

❑ Always let your own staff or your host's assistants attend to all your arrangements, including transportation to and from your hotel.

❑ Dress conservatively and wear well-made suits (see the chapter "What to Wear" for clothing tips).

❑ As the CEO or ranking executive, you are not expected to hold or chair meetings. Your role is to bless the agreements made between the two companies.

❑ Always direct informal discussions with the other side to your counterpart in rank.

❑ Learn a few phrases in Japanese to show you have made the effort to understand Japanese customs. A simple *Dozo yoroshiku* ("It's a pleasure to make your acquaintance") goes a long way.

❑ Let someone else handle the gifts from your company to the Japanese. Make sure the gifts are appropriate, since their quality will be a personal reflection on you as the highest ranked person of your company. (See the chapter "Gift Giving" for more information).

❑ Rank means a lot in Japan, but be careful you are not placed on so high a pedestal that personal connection becomes impossible.

❑   If you are attending a series of formal meetings, plan to attend dinners. Sit in the middle and be prepared to talk a lot during the meal. Dinner talk is usually conducted between the highest ranking executives. Where you may have been quiet during the regular meeting you will be expected to carry the conversation at the dinner. Talk on a very formal level. The Japanese executive may be abstract and vague. Nod politely and try to understand. Raise topics of conversation that are global and industry related, or that involve subjects of obvious mutual interest to your two firms. At very formal dinners the conversation will be mostly between the two higher ups. Everyone else sits and listens patiently. You may want to think in advance about what words of wisdom you have to share or what profound statements of goodwill you want to have heard by those in attendance.

❑   As the highest ranked person you will need to prepare a toast and closing statements.

❑   If you are hosting the dinner let your staff handle the bill and make arrangements to do so before you sit down at the table. Good restaurants in your own country will also allow you to do this.

❑   Remember that you will be viewed as an extension of your firm and that therefore your role is very important in keeping your mutual relations harmonious. Any good or bad feelings at the top will filter down to the staff below and fundamentally affect all your business dealings.

When You Are Solo

There are only two of us in our company. I do all the traveling. On my first visit to our new Japanese clients, we knew it would be tough for us to establish our credibility. So this is what we did. My partner faxed an introduction and we decided that the visit would be "Japanese style"—solely for relationship building. Since I was alone, I contacted an agency in Japan for a translator to accompany me everywhere. I didn't need her skills, but she served as an administrative person for me. Most of my time in Japan was spent reviewing the other company's operations, meeting staff, entertaining, and getting to know the Japanese as individuals. I also extended an invitation to the Japanese to come visit our company in the U.S. It is extremely important that you take the time to establish a close relationship with the Japanese, particularly if you are alone and especially if you are female. (Philadelphia, Pennsylvania)

Most Japanese are aware of the Western business practice of sending a sole negotiator rather than a team. They also realize that the typical Western businesswoman enjoys a higher level of authority than the Japanese businesswoman. Working and visiting in Japan solo, however, is most inconsistent with Japanese culture. The Japanese work in groups and rarely alone. The decision-making process is by way of team consensus. Western thinking promotes the individual as the sole decision maker and many Western businesses position one person to control the entire negotiation. As a Westerner, you may find difficulties because the two business styles are so different. As a female this task can be even harder.

Other problems you may face on your own include awkwardness and isolation. There will always be more than one Japanese person on the other side, and there may be as many as half a dozen depending on the nature of the negotiation. The Japanese side may also send in fresh troops at some point along the way to address other issues. Be sure you get enough rest! Also, with protocol so important, you may feel vulnerable—you could be making a tremendous faux pas and no one would ever tell you about it.

Should you go to Japan on your own?

As a general rule, no. But if you must—or prefer to be solo—take extra precautions.

In Their Own Words

THANKS BUT NO THANKS

On the first day of my first trip to Japan, I was ushered into a separate room to lunch with the OLs ("office ladies"). I thanked my hosts for their thoughtfulness, but told them that I preferred to host a luncheon for them. They declined but, realizing I was uncomfortable being bunched with the OLs, quickly invited me to join them for lunch. (Washington, D.C.)

DISASTER TRIP

Unfortunately on my first trip to Japan I was not told about the keys to doing business there. First, I went alone and was not introduced in advance by my management. Second, I didn't have enough business cards to go around, and they weren't translated into Japanese. Third, I tried to answer all presentation questions even when I didn't know enough specifics. Fourth, I got visibly flustered when my data was questioned because I didn't have good backup information.

As I look back, I realize I didn't come across as a person in charge but as someone trying to do it all. Here is some advice so that others don't have the same bad experience.

- Bring support staff with you or have your subsidiary's colleagues meet you in Japan.

• If support staff is unavailable, have your management advise the Japanese of who you are and that you are traveling alone.

• Bring all your backup documentation, or prepare your home base for late evening phone calls and requests for overnight delivery. (Chicago, Illinois)

BUTT PAT

I always travel alone to our Japanese subsidiary. Over the years, we have worked on many projects together and consider each other to be close associates and friends. On one of my last trips, one of my Japanese colleagues, excited to see me, gave me a hug and a tentative pat on the backside. Startled, I chose to say nothing, thinking it was a momentary mistake on his part. Later the same day, however, a junior engineer, on his way back from the water cooler, gave me a slap on the bottom for no apparent reason, and scurried off without acknowledgement. To put it mildly, I was stunned. I warned my colleague not to repeat those kinds of familiarities, and insisted that he advise the junior engineer likewise. (Mountain View, California)

SOLO AT A SUBSIDIARY

I go solo to our Japan subsidiary over six times a year. I think I've established good working relationships with my counterparts there. To develop and nurture these relationships I make myself available for luncheons and dinners with my colleagues. I also hang around at the office past 5:00 p.m. several nights out of each visit. Many Japanese employees work late and the office atmosphere becomes more relaxed after hours. This is when the informal channels of communication open more quickly and you can get valuable tips that come in handy.

The disadvantage of going to Japan alone is that you have fewer resources at your fingertips, so when things get difficult you are all alone and it's hard to know who to go to for advice and assistance. So you absolutely have to develop friendships with your Japanese colleagues or staff. The best way to do this is over informal lunches or dinners, and by staying a little longer than usual at the office. (Vancouver, British Columbia)

STRATEGY 1,2,3

There was an individual, I'll call him Mr. S., that presented quite a challenge. We were getting ready for a new worldwide advertising campaign and a core group from many different countries was putting together the strategy. We decided on the major theme and I was put in charge of graphics. I'd spent a month working on several possible mock-ups to present at an upcoming meeting.

At the meeting, Mr. S. started to present his own ideas for the campaign, graphics and all. Some of "his" ideas were my ideas—the very ones I had discussed with him two weeks ago on the phone. This was a very critical situation, because it undermined my ability to do my job.

Later, after I got this all sorted out, my Japanese friend and I came up with an analysis of how to react in similar situations. Basically, there are three scenarios to consider:

(1) Is the person usurping your authority your equal?

Politely confront the situation on the spot and respond with the facts, calmly and precisely. Say something like, "At our last joint meeting on August 10, we all agreed that it was my job to research the graphics for this project and that is what my group and I have been working on. Please explain." Regardless of the answer you get, this will establish your authority and force the guilty party to come up with a reasonable explanation other than the perhaps hidden, sexist one of discounting your ability because you're female. Failure to confront the situation right then and there will only result in many more similar kinds of problems.

(2) Is the person usurping your authority your superior?

Say nothing at the meeting. Later on make an appointment to speak privately. Say something like, "I wanted to speak with you in private about the last meeting. I'm not sure what's going on." In other words, keep this open and nonjudgmental, and present yourself as a questioner seeking clarification. If you find the explanation unsatisfactory, say something like, "This makes things very difficult for me to carry out my responsibilities. I hope we can avoid this and similar misunderstandings in the future. But thank you for discussing this with me." Then leave. You've said enough.

(3) Is the person usurping your authority doing so with his own superior present?

This means you have a problem with both the individual and the superior. Say something like what I recommend in the first scenario, but with a bit more formal, polite tone. Then, escalate the problem immediately. Have your boss speak to the Japanese superior.

This may all seem unnecessarily complicated, but soon it will become second nature to you. (Berkeley, California)

STRONG SUIT

Being sent on a solo mission to Japan is tough.

I was sent by my firm to negotiate a new contract with a new vendor. The advice from a colleague I received before I went was a lifesaver. In Japan, the group takes precedence over the individual, which means a solo dealer is not the strong suit. Given this, I was advised to get to know a Japanese individual—even if it was someone from another company and even if he was a customer or a vendor or a partner—that I could discuss matters with informally.

I also tried to break the stigma of "you" versus "me" as quickly as possible by dealing with both sides' issues—I not only developed my own positions but presented possible concerns to the Japanese about their positions. The negotiations soon became quite detailed and non-confrontational, and in my informal discussions with my special Japanese contact, a great deal of inside information and advice came my way. It was more like we were coworkers than two separate companies working out a contract. (Los Angeles, California)

TWO ARE BETTER THAN ONE

My company does consulting, and one of our top consultants is a Chinese-American woman who probably knows more about the Japanese and their language and culture than they do. But because she's Asian, I have to send her to Japan with a "chaperone," in actuality her male subordinate. This is not a reflection on her but on Japanese attitudes toward Asian women. I would never dream of actually replacing her with a man, because she is the best I've got. I have another consultant, a Caucasian woman who is tall, blond, very East Coast. She doesn't need anyone else in Japan because the Japanese look at her and figure she's a no-nonsense female. (Honolulu, Hawaii)

Dos and Don'ts

❑ If you are traveling to Japan alone or for the first time, ask your management to introduce you via fax or letter and follow up with a phone call. Make sure they highlight your responsibilities and title.

❑ If you are a two-person or a small firm, have your partner introduce you via fax.

❑ If you are a sole proprietorship, consider sending in advance a video tape of yourself and your company.

❑ If possible, find a female colleague, secretary, or translator to accompany you on your first trip. A male may be mistaken as your superior.

❑ Establish and confirm all appointments before you go. Never show up unannounced. Have your appointments reconfirmed by a third party or an interpreter after you arrive.

❑ If a conflict or problem arises during your visit, and you need help, enlist a Japanese person to act on your behalf.

❑ Don't let yourself be entertained by the "office ladies" at the Japanese company. These women are not your colleagues. Graciously decline and offer an alternative.

❑ Don't try to answer all the questions if you don't have all the answers. Don't present yourself as a jack of all trades. Don't try to fix every problem by yourself. Answer questions in your area of expertise and responsibility, and follow up on the rest either by phone or when you return to your home base. Be prompt with your answers.

❑ When you travel alone make sure you schedule in phone time with your home office. You may need to review what happened at your meeting more often than do teams who travel.

❑ If you are alone and need to take a lunch break, invite your guests out or have it catered in. Allow the caterer to do everything. Do not serve food yourself.

❏ Get plenty of rest, as you will be "on" all the time and working with many people during your visit.

❏ As a solo visitor you may get considerably more attention than other women travelers, particularly as regards your hotel and transportation needs. It is up to you as to whether you wish to accept any of these courtesies. They can be a very pleasant relief during your travel.

❏ When you are alone you may find that your hosts are less likely to spend social time with you during the evening. They may feel uncomfortable socializing with a lone business female. Be prepared for this and don't push where you're not wanted. Once the relationship is established this awkwardness will go away.

❏ Your Japanese counterparts may arrange special tourist trips for you with a car and guide/interpreter. Although the Japanese probably won't want to join you, by all means politely accept these gestures and enjoy yourself.

❏ If the Japanese firm is coming to visit you they will most likely come as a group. If you are meeting them alone, try to have your secretary and some office personnel join you in the room to help balance the number of attendees. If you are truly a sole proprietorship greet your guests and meet with them alone. Seat them in the same manner you would if you were with a group. See "Business Seating Charts" at the back of this book.

When Your Boss Is Japanese

The first question I was asked by my Japanese boss-to-be was "When do you plan to have children?" Needless to say, I was struck dumb. My first reaction was silent fury and an unsuccessful attempt to come up with a lecturette on sexism. I ended up skirting the question politely with "Well, at present, I am focusing on my career." I was also asked, in this interview and again in many more settings, "What does your husband do?" "How long have you been married?" "What will you do when you have children?" and "How many children do you plan to have?" (Horsham, England)

In the past decade many more Westerners have begun working with Japanese bosses. Many Westerners, attracted by the strength of the Japanese economy and the benefits of being a foreign hire in Japan have moved to Tokyo and Osaka and hired themselves on to Japanese companies. In America, many Japanese companies have expanded their operations and brought in American managers to run them—although the top management and the home office representatives are inevitably Japanese.

The result of all this hiring activity is that many more women are not simply negotiating with the Japanese but working for them. The complication here is obvious—as long as you're working for the American company the Japanese will recognize your "otherness," and this "otherness" will often work to your advantage. But as an employee you have little protection. The law against sexual harassment in Japan is vague and in any case unenforced. In the U.S. you have legal protection, but by the time you decide to use it your work relationship with your Japanese boss has probably gone too far.

As inappropriate as the questions in this chapter's opening vignette may have been, they are standard practice in Japan. Women routinely quit work when pregnant and managers feel it is their duty to keep informed of such developments. We even know of one secretary who got a cash bonus just because she was pregnant. Of course, she was also expected to quit work immediately after she made public her condition. Our advice to women seeking work in a Japanese company or seeking work where your boss is a Japanese male is to be prepared for these kinds of probing personal questions and either do what the woman above did or give a more culturally informed answer, stating simply that you know such questions are routine in Japan and that the manager is probably concerned about how long you plan to work. Then say, "But I am a professional woman who has chosen a career and I keep my personal and professional life separate."

One additional problem you may have—and this may surprise you—is that your relationship with other Japanese women working for the same company will be strained. You will probably be getting paid more than they are, and you may have more responsibility. If you are an expatriate hire working in Japan, you will have numerous stipends and benefits that local hires will not. Some of the problems may simply come down to the fact that you're assertive and stand up for your rights, whereas many of the Japanese women may want to but fail to out of fear and conditioning. Management may use "sisterhood" against you—insisting that you come in early to sweep up and boil tea water with the other "girls"—or you may feel the pressure to go along with sexist policies out of fear of embarrassing your Japanese female colleagues.

Our advice: be true to yourself and let your example lead others. You may work for a Japanese company and perhaps even be of Japanese descent, but you're *not* culturally Japanese. The Japanese women in your company likely have their own priorities. The reason for their inaction may be more complex than you realize. Taking a stand, in their view, may not be worth the isolation and repercussions it produces. By acting in accordance with your own beliefs, you will be in a better position to play an effective role in the Japanese company. You may even find that others will solicit your advice and help. Remember that working in small but incremental ways is much more effective, in the long run, than bold,, one-time stances.

Jn Their Own Words

FIRST MEETING WITH MY BOSS

I wish someone had told me what to expect at my first meeting with my Japanese boss. It was different.

The meeting took an hour and he said nothing about anything relevant to my experience, my qualifications, or anything—not even a hint of the usual Japanese worries about how long I, as a woman, intended to work before starting a family. Mostly we chatted about the differences in education between Europe, America, and Japan, and then about the advantages and disadvantages of reading multi-national newspapers. I didn't know what he wished to accomplish, what he expected of me, how long I should continue the small talk, etc. Simply put, I had no clue what the meeting was all about.

I wish someone had told me that that was a typical first meeting, that at a get-acquainted session shoptalk is always excluded. The employee is expected to follow the boss's lead, and it would be the height of rudeness to cut the conversation short on one's own. The boss will end the chat when he feels the time is right. I don't have the faintest clue what impression I gave that first meeting. I must have scratched my head at least fifty times and looked bewildered to the end. (Atlanta, Georgia)

KEEP COOL

Japanese work better with those who don't cause a lot of turbulence. If you know you are a high-energy person, maybe you shouldn't work for the Japanese. Women usually have to struggle to be heard, so at home they're used to environments that allow them to assert themselves more than their male counterparts do. This is not looked on favorably in Japanese firms. There, you should speak slowly, listen with interest, and make your point with deference, not disagreement—whether you're male or female. (Tokyo, Japan)

LOW-TECH AND CEREMONIES

Unlike the products they make, Japanese firms are really quite low-tech. Their work style involves a lot of daytime communications and then a lot of evening work when the Tokyo offices are open. Japanese firms don't like individual "stars"; if you need to stand out or need lots of reinforcement, don't work for the Japanese. Don't expect individual recognition. Don't expect immediate feedback. Do expect to have to participate in lots of ceremonies, functions, and dinners. (Orange County, California)

IS THIS FORMAL OR INFORMAL?

Anyone on business in Japan better know the big difference between formal and informal business situations.

I first met Mr. Ota, my Japanese vice president of finance, at a company social function. He was talkative, casual, outgoing, and even told a joke or two—good ones, at that. I felt right at home chatting with him. The next day I arrived at his office fifteen minutes early for a meeting. At the exact time of our scheduled appointment, Mr. Ota opened the door to his office and said, "Please come in." Then, taking his seat behind the desk, we got right down to business. No smiles. No chitchat. Nothing but business for the whole hour. I don't think he even recognized me from the night before.

I started wondering "What was I wearing last night?" "Do I look that different today?" "Maybe he is unhappy with my performance?" "Is there something I should be following up on?" "Maybe I offended him last night?" I was really concerned.

But I learned that there was nothing weird about this. In Japan, formal business behavior and informal social behavior are clearly delineated. (San Francisco, California)

TEA, WHAT TO DO WITH THE TEA?

When I first went to work for a Japanese company in Osaka, months of cross-cultural training didn't prevent me from being horrified at the prospect of being asked to serve tea. True, tea is primarily the responsibility of the OLs or "office ladies," but after a while on the job, I noticed that everyone at the company was serving tea, even the men. So it didn't seem like such a big deal after all. I didn't want to make myself out to be someone special. "The nail that sticks up gets hammered down," as the Japanese saying goes. (Osaka, Japan)

TEA AND EMPATHY

I started serving tea from the first week I joined my Japanese company. The other women were doing it and I felt for me to refuse would be somehow an insult to them. I then quickly learned that serving tea was not all they were doing. The women all came in a half hour earlier than everyone else to dust tables, straighten the desks and chairs, and get the morning tea ready to go. Somehow all this had escaped my notice during the hustle and bustle of my first week. Well, what to do? I told my boss that I just could not participate in this kind of sexist behavior. he asked me to think about how my refusing would affect the other women. What would they think? How would they feel? I went away and thought about it. I then returned to my boss and said that I still couldn't engage in such a discriminating practice. The result of this was that everyone—men and women—had to start dusting and tea brewing. I had caused a mini-revolution. Actually it was chaotic, and the worst part was that I couldn't get a sense of how it really made the women feel. Of course the *bucho* (department head) insisted on having his tea served anyway since he was "just too old to change." I'm not sure how this will play out. I wish I could fast forward a few months and see where it all leads. The most important thing for me out of all this, though, is the empathy I feel for the Japanese women I work with. I'm still trying to work out my role in conjunction with theirs, and believe me it's not easy. (Tokyo, Japan)

ACTION PLAN

Get used to getting asked a lot of detailed questions and giving detailed answers. Make sure you have plenty of data to back you up. Don't expect an immediate reaction. You may have to wait a month or more, but your presentation ideas won't be forgotten. If you're a subordinate, you'll most likely have a lot of tasks just abruptly dumped on you by your higher ups. Subordinates in general in Japan are not treated with much ceremony, so be sure you don't confuse being a subordinate with being treated poorly because you're a woman. (Melbourne, Australia)

TAKE-CHARGE APPROACH

I've worked over ten years for Japanese firms in the U.S. The key to success in my opinion is to develop honest and good relationships with the Japanese. They're quite nervous at first about working with women. They'll take a wait-and-see approach. In general, Japanese men are shy. They have a distrust of Westerners, and lots of doubts about the role of women in the workplace. Contrary to popular belief, though, you're not just a token foreigner unless you set yourself up as such. I suggest a take charge approach. This may be treated with silence at first as the Japanese adapt to you, but later you'll find it is to your benefit. (Long Island, New York)

INDIRECT COMMUNICATION

You can tell how well you're doing in a Japanese company by the amount of responsibility you're given. The more the better. If responsibility is withdrawn the Japanese think you are not achieving. If communication stops, something is definitely wrong. It's up to you to initiate a conversation about the problem, but you have to talk about something unrelated to it first. You may never really learn what set them off. The important thing though is to break through the silence barrier and relieve whatever anger they're feeling. But remember, it's a serious flaw in Japanese eyes if you try to bullshit them or flatly lie. (Seattle, Washington)

IT'S TOUGH FOR THE JAPANESE MAN

The Japanese men are constantly being rotated. They come here as Japanese nationals and stay long enough to figure out their job, and then they're sent back to Japan and replaced by greenhorns who will make the same mistakes all over again. During the transition period there's no decision making. It's hard for the men. They get to prefer the Western style of on-the-spot decision making and still end up getting caught in Japanese-style consensus building. They want to be Westerners, but they have to hold onto their Japanese ways. Many of them don't want to go back to Japan. But they have no choice. (Denver, Colorado)

ADVICE MAN

I called him "Advice Man." When I started working for a Japanese company he was the one individual who took it upon himself to give me advice about everything. He would critique my clothing, my memo writing, my participations at meetings. Just about everything I did he had some piece of advice to "help me" with.

At first I wanted to know everything and anything and welcomed his tips, but what started as friendly criticism later became a put-you-in-your-place put-down. After a few months, needless to say, I wanted this "advice" to stop.

At first, I thought of discussing the problem with my boss but was advised not to. So I decided to ask other Japanese colleagues and at the same time let them know how very unhappy I was about what this man was doing. I got some good advice. I was told that everyone had noticed his derogatory comments to me and that the next time it happened I should publicly say something like, "Mr. S, I appreciate your desire to help me but I don't need your advice. Please don't waste our time with unnecessary comments, and if I have a question about something I will ask for your assistance." The very next time he piped up I did exactly that. I no longer have Mr. Advice Man breathing down my neck and life has improved greatly. (Cupertino, California)

PROS AND CONS

As a Western woman, working for a Japanese firm can be a great experience. It's cross-cultural, and you can learn a lot. Women working for Japanese companies in the U.S. especially can get good positions, since the companies have to hire minorities and local workers. The best thing is to have a special skill or specialization, since there's no future for you with the Japanese if you're just a clerk or secretary. Asian-American women have it more difficult since they have an Asian face but a Western upbringing. Japanese men look at them and expect them to act like Japanese women. An Asian-American woman is more likely to be asked to serve tea. When it comes to women and men of color, the Japanese have a real prejudice. It's very sad, and unjustified. (New York City, New York)

YOU WOULD BE HAPPIER STAYING HOME WITH YOUR BABY

An expectant mother as well as a highly regarded secretary, I'll call her Michiko, wanted to continue working after delivery. She requested a maternity leave of six months. Our company was a U.S. subsidiary in Tokyo, but our human resource manager was Japanese.

Before her meeting with Human Resources, Michiko received a letter from her American boss expressing his high esteem for her as a valued employee, and specifying that he would be more than glad to hire temporary staff until she could return to work. Michiko took this letter to her meeting with the HR manager. At the meeting, however, she was told about all the advantages of staying home to care for the baby, and was reassured that she would be happier at home not worrying about the pressures of work. Michiko politely reiterated her original intentions and the manager apparently relented, promising to consider her request.

Of course I was angry when Michiko told me about the meeting. But I was even more outraged when I heard through the grapevine that the manager was already interviewing for her permanent replacement. Michiko was about to give up. In Japan, the pressure to quit work when pregnant is enormous, and she was getting it from all sides—family, friends, and employer. I decided to lend a hand and speak to the manager, very politely, about Michiko. He told me that there wasn't a company policy for maternity leave and in any case he had no time to write it. Realizing I was wasting my time, I decided to take Michiko's case up with the Human Resources people in the U.S. They saw the potential for a lawsuit and settled the matter immediately. Michiko is now a happy mother and a happy career secretary. (Tokyo, Japan)

BEER BUST, YOUR BUST

It was Friday night in Osaka and my company was hosting a beer bust in the executive lounge of our Japanese subsidiary. A Japanese colleague and I were making small talk, sharing anecdotes about our experiences working with foreign companies, when for no apparent reason he says, "Beer Bust," looks meaningfully at my breasts, and laughs.

This is a typical example of bad Japanese male humor with non-native members of the opposite sex. You should either respond with silence to such jokes or walk away. If the joking continues you should warn the guy that sexual harassment laws apply even in Japan, especially to those working in U.S. companies. Be direct about it, and say, "You should be aware of the sexual harassment policies of our company. In case you need to review them, I'll make sure you get a copy by next week at the latest. In the meantime, it's not OK for you to speak like you just did to me or to any woman in our company."

Correct the problem on the spot and don't wait until later when you might be even angrier. If you act fast, you can still preserve the business relationship. I should add that I sensed relief from many of the Japanese males after this incident. It was as if I had drawn the line, and now it was more clear to them how to treat me. (Palo Alto, California)

WORK HARD, PLAY HARD
Working hours at a Japanese company are longer, and socializing is really important. If you are a woman, yes, learn to play golf. I have seen men of lesser caliber get ahead because they play golf. I know it sounds silly, but tennis is another good sport to learn. (Santa Clara, California)

GETTING FEEDBACK
I'd rate how to get feedback from your Japanese boss the number one difficulty. They just don't give feedback to employees in the same way as American bosses do. The reason for this, I have learned, is that praise is seen as unnecessary. "A good employee doesn't need praise" is what I was told. It is only children who need strokes. An adult knows whether what he or she is doing is right. This thinking made good sense to me, but it had consequences I wasn't prepared for. Since a Japanese boss doesn't give praise, when he does comment on your performance it's all negative. This can be a big shocker.

There's more you should know about this. It's assumed that a good employee will ask for assistance, guidance, and suggestions. I had to learn this the hard way, by trial and error. I had worked hard on a presentation and I didn't even think my boss knew anything about it. Wrong. When it came time to give the presentation, there he was sitting in the back—just showed up out of nowhere. Time stood still for me the whole time I was talking. After the presentation my boss vanished. Back at the office he said nothing. I waited. Nothing. Finally, a week and a half later, I made an appointment to speak with him. In his office I politely asked for his comments on my presentation. He rummaged through a pile of papers and retrieved seven pages of comments he had prepared for me. And yes, eighty percent was what I could do better. Years later I've come to appreciate this manager's style. (Berkeley, California)

CONSOLIDATED, MOVED, DOCKED, GONE

I was with my company for almost ten years. The first four years were quite good. The company was starting up in the U.S. and there was an overwhelming need to establish itself, so money was no object. But five years ago they brought new people in, older more conservative types who maybe didn't cotton to women running things (at the time I was in charge of three departments). First they wanted to "consolidate" operations and take one of the departments away from me. Then everything I proposed had to be verified against what other companies were doing. Then they started hiring lots of Western men, and you can imagine what they were like—nobody good wanted to work for us, so we pulled in the dregs. These men were brought in at the top and given good pay, but they brought all their old, lousy attitudes with them, very much in line with the all too prevalent anti-woman opinions of the Japanese. I ended up being placed under one of these men, and then the entire organization was disbanded. Finally I was placed under a Japanese national, who turned out to be extremely supportive. He let me develop a new department, but when his rotation was up he confided that I should look elsewhere. He said he had had to spend a lot of time protecting me, but once he was gone it would all be over. Sure enough, he left and my secretary was taken away. I had a medical leave, and when I came back I found my pay had been cut over twelve percent. We found out that only women and no men were having their pay reduced, and that this was happening in the finance department as well. Those women ended up staging a walkout and going to HR when they were told that henceforth they had to bring a male to every meeting since women were too prone to become "emotional" in business.

Although I'm very grateful for the one Japanese man who was truly an enlightened soul, I regretfully must give the following advice: The best way to deal with Japanese firms is to enter, learn what they have to teach you about intercultural business dealings, get some perspective, and then get out. (Alameda, California)

Dos and Don'ts

❏ Japanese value graduates of prestigious universities. If your background is strong academically, be sure to emphasize this in your interviews.

❏ Learn the difference between formal and informal business protocol. Pleasant times you enjoy after hours may not carry over at all to the next business day.

❏ Don't confuse politeness with friendship.

❏ Stay flexible in your job responsibilities and don't try to immediately define your job description. It will take a good six months for the parameters of your job to become clear to you. In Japanese companies many things never get made explicit and hardly ever in writing. Clear-cut job descriptions are one of them.

❏ Salary at a Japanese company in Japan always involves more than just the monthly salary. Look at bonuses, housing, transportation stipends, pension plans, and health care.

❏ The "information loop" at a Japanese company is usually hard for a foreigner to join. Especially in the U.S., real decision-making power is often retained by Tokyo and communicated to the overseas staff by late-night phone calls or faxes in Japanese. Spend time socializing with key Japanese personnel to find out what's really happening at your company.

❏ Especially if you are working in Japan, try to learn Japanese if you plan to work for a Japanese firm. Knowing the language is considered an asset and you will be respected for making the effort.

❑ A boss is always a boss—observe the hierarchy at all times, even when everyone's had a few drinks and is feeling friendly.

❑ Don't ever embarrass your boss publicly. Don't contradict him in public. Give your input, if you disagree, in private.

❑ Don't complain to your boss about another employee. Instead, present the facts you are sure of minus your personal feelings about the individual.

❑ Bring up your personal concerns to your boss in a one-on-one session. Make your needs known in the form of a suggestion.

❑ It is up to you, the employee, to ask for advice or feedback from the boss. Don't be surprised if most of what you hear is negative. Japanese bosses are not famous for dishing out the praise.

❑ Resignation is a big deal in Japan and is not treated lightly. Respect the Japanese efforts to put a good face on a bad situation.

❑ Any kind of emotionalism is completely unprofessional and will most likely undermine your authority.

❑ Japanese are punctual in the morning and often hesitate to leave at night when others are staying behind. When you're late coming in or leaving the office early, simply say "I'm sorry" and leave it at that. Any more will sound like you're just making excuses.

❑ Keep your personal life out of the business environment in Japan more than you would at home—at least in the beginning. Personal phone calls at work should be saved for your lunch hour or restricted to very brief messages.

❑ Right from the beginning, don't tolerate any kind of sexual harassment. It is up to you to draw the line.

The Woman's Advantage

The greatest advantage I have being a woman is that I can network at many more levels than my male counterparts. In a tightly structured society like Japan's that is much more hierarchical than our own, matching rank, or titles, is very important. Communication happens with your counterpart and you are pretty much confined to network at your own level. It is difficult for a male director from my company to talk to an engineer on the Japanese team, for example. Being a woman on business in Japan, however, you are considered something of an oddity and an outsider, so you don't have to observe such strict lines of communication. You must work harder at first to establish yourself as credible, but you can then use your outsider status to your benefit. You can be a very valuable information source for your team because the communication channels from the secretary all the way on up are accessible to you. It is an indispensable negotiating advantage. (Tokyo, Japan)

Up to now we've been talking about the problems of being a woman and working with the Japanese. The *advantages* of being a woman and working with the Japanese are still a well-guarded secret.

First, you get noticed. You are perhaps a somewhat unsettling presence, but by the same token you are always a presence to be reckoned with. You just have to make sure that the attention you get is the kind you want.

Second, once the initial, sometimes difficult steps are taken and your authority is established, you are generally perceived as more understanding and sympathetic than your male colleagues. Therefore don't overdo the formal professional image—strike a comfortable compromise between professional and friendly. If you do this, a lot of the nitty-gritty, otherwise hard-to-get information finds its way, or gets fed, to you. (The difficulty here is that, once you have established the working relationship, you spend a great deal of time at business luncheons, dinners, and late-night phone calls to your home office.)

Third, as a woman you can be much more flexible than your male colleagues, because—as we have seen above—you can network at just about all levels of the Japanese organization.

And fourth, and best of all, you can be a lot more direct in expressing the pros and cons of your business interests than can the Western male. This last point may be a surprise to you, but here's what we mean: The Japanese career woman is not expected to take part in the male-oriented nightlife—where a lot of informal business decisions are made—so all her communicating must be done at the office. Forced to be a lot more direct in her communication style than her Japanese male colleagues, she has, accordingly, built up a no-nonsense female image, an image which can apply to you too. Follow her lead and you will have a tremendous advantage. By presenting yourself as someone with authority, know-how, and cultural understanding, you can get a great deal more accomplished than most of your male coworkers.

In Their Own Words

SOLUTION FINDERS

I think women, especially American women, excel in negotiations with the Japanese. As a rule, we are more patient and accepting of Japanese business protocol in meetings than our male colleagues. We like to spend time discussing the proposal or problem until everyone understands and agrees. We tend not to raise our voices or argue, and therefore can more easily find areas of agreement. We're viewed as solution finders, and can break through impasses. Some of my male colleagues, on the other hand, jump in with an idea, try to take over the meeting, and expect immediate cooperation. They set themselves up to fail. The argumentative approach inevitably gets the silent treatment from the Japanese, damaging the relationship and prolonging the meetings. (Vancouver, British Columbia)

INTUITION PAYS OFF

I feel that as a woman I've been able to be more sensitive to the give and take of Japanese communication styles than my male colleagues. I can read between the lines and respond in ways that make the Japanese more comfortable, men and women alike. We women are prompt, pay attention to details, are willing to listen—and we're intuitive. Many Western men don't seem to have or value these qualities. The Japanese and I work well together in business. When we have a large business problem, we resolve it outside the business meeting setting through a series of phone calls and faxes and bring the resolution to the table. This is an effective way of doing business in a consensus society like Japan's. (Knoxville, Tennessee)

THE ROYAL TREATMENT

Yes, there are advantages to being a women in business. I didn't know how I'd be received on my first visit to Japan. To my delight, I was given the red carpet treatment. My male predecessor had been escorted to bars and nightclubs until all hours of the night. I was treated differently. I was taken to the finest restaurants in the area and to a tea ceremony. A car, interpreter, and guide were arranged for me over the weekend for sightseeing. Whenever I go to Japan, I'm treated like a visiting dignitary. (Santa Clara, California)

ESTABLISH THE RELATIONSHIP

True, it's harder for women at first, but on the other hand women in general are less politically inclined than Western men are. Western men tend to develop good-old-boy kinds of networks. And men can't seem to grasp the respect and relationship concept. They have a hard time getting to know the Japanese management. They are used to getting attention and the spotlight, and they want to move ahead too quickly. They don't know how to listen, or to be patient. They tend to break the harmony of the meeting, until it all breaks down. But women can be direct and they can listen too. This is the key to trust. I remember I spent an average of two nights a week, every week, having dinners with my manager and getting to know him personally. And it was at these dinners that I really first started to find out what was going on at the firm. I've had a very good relationship with my boss, and I most of all appreciate the time he spends communicating to me. I have never had this kind of attention from any Western manager. (Dallas, Texas)

SINGLED OUT

I was the only female engineer on the team. When we arrived at one of the customer sites in Japan, my male colleague asked to see a high-security area of the plant. He was refused permission. Later I expressed the same interest, and it was arranged. When I got to know my Japanese counterpart better, I asked why I had been allowed to see the area while my male colleague hadn't. He said that, since I was the only woman on the team, the risk of a leak could be kept low. Had they shown the high-security area to a man, they would then have been obligated to show it to the entire American team. (Ipponmatsu, Japan)

THE OLDER THE BETTER

I'm—well—close to sixty, let's say. I've been working with Japan for some thirty years and the older I've gotten the easier it gets. I get instant respect and none of the difficulties younger women sometimes do. I speak Japanese, I'm involved in high-level negotiations for my company, and thoroughly enjoy my business trips to Japan. I've learned to relax and appreciate the relationships I've built up over the years. What I like most is that, once you know the rules of the game, things are clear and predictable. You know what to do and what to expect. It is a lot more clear-cut in Japan and I enjoy that clarity. (Santa Clara, California)

Dos and Don'ts

❏ As a Western woman be direct in your communication during business discussions.

❏ Don't confuse being direct with being confrontational. You can imply "You messed up" without saying "You messed up." For example, you can say, "This doesn't meet the requirements discussed at our last meeting. Could you please explain?" Women are more adept and diplomatic when it comes to polite advisements than Western men are. This is a real advantage in Japan, where it sometimes pays to be a little long-winded when giving bad news.

❏ Use your ability as a woman to network at many different levels throughout the Japanese organization. Women report that since they are good listeners and relationship builders they are generally more effective at doing this than Western men.

❏ Don't give your home phone number to just anyone. This may attract an unwanted relationship or it will inevitably result in business extending into your private time on an all-too-regular basis.

❏ As a woman you may be more patient than your male counterparts. This can be critical in Japanese meetings, which tend to go on forever with much repetition and clarification of points.

❏ You may have more kindnesses and courtesies—such as an escort around town—offered you than your male colleagues. Since women in business are still something new for the Japanese they may react toward you with overpoliteness and some special handling. Enjoy the extra hospitality, as long as it doesn't interfere with the job.

❏ As a woman you can decline to go to the after-hours social events (where you would be uncomfortable anyway; see the chapter "Socializing There"). Take advantage of this to do what you want to do and to get a good night's rest.

❑ Women are perceived as mediators by the Japanese. Use this perception to create a stronger partnership with your counterparts. This advantage is especially valuable during tough negotiations or business transactions.

❑ The Japanese rely on intuition and sensitivity to achieve unspoken understanding of difficult situations, especially those involving people and relationships. These traits are also highly developed in many Western women, and this gives them a special advantage when dealing with Japan.

What to Wear

Well, call me vain but I have to admit I look forward to putting together my business wardrobe. When the hemlines came up and colors hit the major boutiques, guess who was first in line? Female fashion designers have introduced us to above-the-knee suits, collector pants, and fresh textures. But you'll see none of this on Japanese female professionals. So when I pack for Japan, I go to the depths of my closet and pull out, much to the protestation of my own sense of good taste, navy suits, gray suits, and high-collared blouses. It reminds me of college "interview" days—less the bow tie. That was when women felt the need to emulate men to be accepted as corporate comrades. What a relief things have changed! The key is adapting. I'm not about to jeopardize my credibility over "steel" leather suits, animal prints, military accents, or even the to-die-for magenta pants coordinate. My career is too important. To me it's all just another chess game, where the queen has the flexibility and moves and the king is so limited. If played well, the queen will always win the game. (Milan, Italy)

The managerial-track career woman, *kyaria uman*, is still not a significant part of corporate Japan, but she does exist. The most visible females in the Japanese business environment, however, are the OLs ("office ladies") that exclusively fill the administrative and clerical positions. OLs and the *kyaria uman* dress completely differently. As a foreign businesswoman, you should always dress like the *kyaria uman*, never like the OL.

OLs enter the workplace in their early twenties and leave shortly after marriage to start a family. Japanese women almost invariably marry by the age of twenty-five. The current slang term for a single woman over twenty-five is "Christmas Cake"—which means that, like day-old holiday pastry, no one wants a "stale" bride. The social pressure to get married is enormous, and if the young working woman doesn't succeed on her own her office manager will probably take time during the working day to show her pictures of eligible bachelors who work for the company. She makes her choices, goes on arranged dates with one or more of the prospects, and reports her preferences to the boss and other concerned parties.

In the Japanese scheme of things, once the working woman accepts such introductions it is hard, if not impossible, to back out of the process graciously. As a result, increasing numbers of women are postponing or forgoing the whole procedure altogether, including the institution of marriage. This trend alarms Japanese men, because it significantly restricts their access to pools of eligible women. Most women, however, sooner or later succumb to societal pressures and exit the workforce, thus making way for younger and cheaper workers to staff the OL position.

Since the OL is fresh out of high school or college and still lives at home, her income is almost entirely discretionary. Much of it goes into clothes and accessories for the office. As a rule, these are expensive, always fashionable, and sometimes trendy or "flashy." Because she knows she will never be a part of the mainstream business world, she dresses largely as she pleases.

The *kyaria uman*, on the other hand, projects an entirely different picture from the temporary, expendable OL. She is part of the mainstream Japanese business world, but because this has traditionally been a male preserve she is still very much an oddity and must present herself as one hundred percent business and nothing else. She wears no jewelry except for a watch and simple ring—and little or no makeup. No fancy clothing here, only conservative suits and low heels.

In Their Own Words

THE POWER SUIT

I would say that the decision about what to wear on your business trip to Japan, like anywhere else, depends on the image you want to project. I am a single businesswoman, young by Japanese standards, and I've been told I'm "most likely to get hit on" by Japanese males. So for me conservative business suits are a must. I do not wear pant suits when I am visiting Japan. The skirt suit is a more "powerful" uniform. My female colleagues who are engineers, on the other had, have no problem with pant suits—especially when they have to go to traditional restaurants and sit on tatami mats. (New York City, New York)

HE TOLD ME WHAT TO WEAR!

I was planning to visit one of our expatriates in Japan. I wrote him to confirm the agenda for some of our upcoming meetings. His return correspondence included details on what I should wear. I was furious. I have a Ph.D., I'm of Asian decent, and I know how to conduct myself in any Far Eastern business environment. When I expressed my irritation, he pointed out that many professional women visitors from our U.S. offices had come to Japan dressed very inappropriately. They had worn trendy dresses and shoes, too much makeup, elaborate costume jewelry, and evening wear for dinner. My colleague just wanted to help, and since he was unaware of my Asian background, he assumed I would make the same mistakes. (San Jose, California)

LOW CUT, NO GO

"Western women have big breasts and it is very hard not to look at them." I was told this once by a Japanese colleague, and the second part of his sentence appears to be true. I don't recommend wearing any low-cut or tight-fitting clothes in Japan. Once I had to go to several customer sites in the month of August—always a hot and humid time of year in Japan. So for my comfort I wore a low-cut blouse with my usual business suit. Everyone stared straight at my chest, especially on the trains. I now wear only high-collared or mandarin-styled blouses. (Atlanta, Georgia)

NO LOVE HERE

I remember when an American woman was making a presentation in Japan on Valentine's Day. Because of the occasion she wore red. In Japan, however, they do not wear red on Valentine's Day and they certainly don't wear it on business. It's too provocative. The woman's Japanese audience reacted to her with shock and just sat and stared. Not only was the attire inappropriate, it was taken as an insult. (Milpitas, California)

ATTENTION!

When I go to Japan, I take two suits—one charcoal gray, the other navy blue. I have them dry cleaned every night and alternate wearing them during my visit. I bring button covers, various blouses, and a few stickpins to vary the look. But that's it. My suits are all conservative. I wear low-heel black shoes, carry an attache case, and wear just a watch. Since I'm usually surrounded by much more casually dressed engineering staff, I always stand out. I get immediate attention and respect when I walk into the room. There is never a question in the minds of my Japanese counterparts about who is in charge. (Boston, Massachusetts)

Dos and Don'ts

❑ Dress to project a conservative image using suits or dresses with jackets.

❑ Wear charcoal-colored suits, grays, navy blues, greens, and browns.

❑ Wear a well-made, solid-colored suit. A conservative plaid may also be appropriate.

❑ Don't wear red. It is too flashy and sexy.

❑ Wear blouses that are white, cream, pinstriped, or conservatively patterned.

❑ Avoid black. The color alone connotes funeral attire. Break up the color pattern with some color—a blouse, brooch, or scarf.

❑ Don't wear polyester clothes.

❑ Don't wear pastels or florals. They do not project a conservative, professional image.

❑ Don't wear flashy clothing with any gold or silver threads.

❑ Don't wear miniskirts, tight-fitting clothes, or low-cut blouses.

❑ Don't change into formal attire for dinner. Wear your business suit.

❑ Wear good leather shoes in basic black, brown, or navy with medium heels.

❑ Don't wear spiked heels. A 2" heel is best.

❑ Don't wear plastic shoes.

❑ Don't wear casual shoes such as strap or open-toe shoes.

❑ Wear good hosiery. You will be taking off your shoes in many places. Don't wear hosiery that is brightly colored or patterned.

❑ Wear a slip under your suit since you may not be as graceful as you would like when getting up from a tatami mat—your seat in a traditional Japanese restaurant and another reason for wearing a loose skirt.

❑ Wear your hair in a conservative style, not elaborately coiffured.

❑ Carry a handkerchief to pat your face. The humidity can be extreme.

❑ Use a brand-name handbag if you bring one. Handbag brands are keys to status.

❑ Don't wear heavy makeup, perfume, or dark or brightly colored nail polish.

❑ If you are tall, be prepared for a lot of short mirrors and toylike furniture in your Japanese hotel.

❑ Don't wear big or dangling earrings, creative pins, or necklaces. Traditional brooches, wedding rings, and a plain watch are all acceptable jewelry. When visiting conservative Japanese companies, avoid gold necklaces and jewelry that stands out in any way. Pearls are fine to wear, but are considered formal.

❑ In summer, remember that Japan is hot and humid. Linen or lightweight clothes are a good idea.

❑ In June and the fall it is rainy, so bring an umbrella and raincoat.

❑ In winter when it can get cold, wear a wool suit and take gloves and a scarf.

Socializing There

I thought that being invited by the Japanese to their after-hours group outings at the bars and clubs was an honor, a celebration of your personal acceptance. I thought the invitation was a declaration of friendship and a great start to a long-term business relationship. Later I found out that joining the boys is not what I should have done, especially on my first trip. Their invitation was only a formality, and everyone was uncomfortable with my being there. So I think now that, by going out to the clubs and being more relaxed socially, I became less effective in my working relationships. I now politely thank everyone for the invitation but decline. I think everyone is relieved. I reserve after-dinner socializing only for when I truly know my Japanese counterpart, and even then I am cautious. (Paris, France)

Socializing after hours is part and parcel of doing business in Japan— if you're a man. At drinking holes and tiny eateries, businessmen gather, consume great quantities of beer, whiskey, or sake, and gradually loosen some of the formal restrictions that had guided their interactions during the business day. Their tongues loosened too, the men may discuss office politics or new projects. If there are clients and customers they may exchange industry gossip or pitch ideas on how relations between their respective companies can be improved. All of the important proposals, partnerships, and reorganizations in Japan have probably been launched and brainstormed outside of the conventional business setting. After-hours socializing is also where new colleagues get to know each other and feel comfortable, and begin that long and arduous path toward "trust," perhaps the single most important element in any successful Japanese business relationship.

Note that we've been talking about businessmen here. As a woman, you're out of the loop. Because while these same men are discussing business or just getting to know each other, they are in an atmosphere where you would feel completely out of place. These small eateries, pubs, karaoke bars, hostess clubs, and other nightspots are designed exclusively for the entertainment of men. The women who work there may be scantily clad liquor servers, or kimono-clad hostesses whose job it is to fawn over the men, light their cigarettes, keep their glasses full, and engage in suggestive sexual banter. Some are certainly prostitutes.

Given that you're a foreigner, isn't it possible for you to be a foreigner first and a woman second (or not at all?). In this case, it's difficult. Since it is only with "women on the periphery" that a Japanese businessman socializes at night, by going along you suggest a willingness on your part to suspend the normal rules of distance and mutual respect between male and female, and you openly invite the kind of small talk appropriate to a sexual relationship. Also, the liquor makes it more likely for the men—or you—to do or say something that you might be embarrassed thinking about the next day (although the general rule among Japanese is that what goes on at night is not brought back to the office). In brief, you will likely find the bar/club scene uncomfortable, if not downright insulting.

There are simply no benefits in accompanying your group to after-hours establishments that cater only to men. More to the point, after-hours socializing will make it that much harder for you to establish and maintain the authority you need for a successful business relationship. By declining the invitation to participate you avoid making everyone uneasy, you raise the comfort level of your Japanese counterparts by showing them you are in the know, and you get a good night's sleep.

But what do you do if you are invited by the Japanese to join their after-hours nightlife? You go to dinner with them and graciously decline the drinking afterward. Since the serious drinking almost always takes place at a separate venue from the dinner, it is easy to detach yourself from the group and take your own cab back to your hotel. Your "bow out" will be appreciated by your hosts although they may seemingly persist.

We should mention that in our interviews with professional women in numerous fields, we found a great many who felt it was perfectly OK to socialize at the bars and clubs with their Japanese clients. They said that, although they left a bit earlier than the men on their team, they felt there was no disadvantage to joining in on the nighttime entertainment. As authors we realize our policy on this may be a bit conservative, but we strongly believe it is the safest one to recommend. Our advice, in a nutshell, is that it is best not to participate in the drinking and singing that goes on after dinner (going out to dinner itself is fine and expected of you). After-hours reveling can make you less effective in your business dealings. If you must make an exception to this rule, do so after you've truly come to know your Japanese business partners and established a *professional* relationship. If your being a woman is at all an issue, skip the entertainment. Or find colleagues in your own company who will go out with you instead.

One other reason for not heading to the bars: you will be expected to sing, either solo (if you are in a private room, say) or accompanying the karaoke machine. Since it is rude to excuse yourself from this task, come prepared a couple songs you can handle. To make things easier, you can also enlist a colleague to join you in a duet. But be forewarned that some of the videos now accompanying the karaoke are pretty raunchy and will most likely make you uncomfortable. Again, our advice is: don't go.

Now that you're on your own for the evening, how should you spend your time? If you have the energy to go out after working try Kabuki or Noh theater, a city night tour, or other local events that can be arranged through your hotel. You can also try the infinite variety of unique and expensive coffee or snack shops, the jazz *kissa* (jazz clubs) where you can drink espresso and listen to the world's best in jazz recordings, the theater, a movie, the symphony, sumo, and even Japanese baseball. There are also some "women only" clubs, massage parlors, and discotheques, although as a foreigner you may have some trouble finding them. As a rule you should not go out alone, since chances are good that you will be mistaken for an "easy mark" and find a line of men waiting to join you at your table. The exception to this is at the major hotels. If you wish to unwind after dinner over a few drinks, go to the bar in your hotel or any of the other major hotels and you will not be bothered. Note too that personal safety on the trains and streets at night is very good just about everywhere you'll be going in Japan, so don't let that worry keep you indoors.

In Their Own Words

THE BUSINESS LUNCH
I was in Japan at our subsidiary and wanted to continue a business discussion with my Japanese counterpart. It was approaching 12:30, so I invited him out to lunch. He agreed, but acted like a completely different person during the meal—uptight and strained. I later learned he was embarrassed because I had invited him out alone, and had made the invitation in front of others in his department. I had put him in a very difficult position, and subjected him to merciless taunting by his peers. As a rule, don't invite a Japanese man out alone. Invite someone to join you and, at least, make it a threesome. (Berkeley, California)

HOSPITALITY PLUS!
The Japanese are extremely hospitable to visitors. I discovered that on what I had hoped to be a short visit to a firm. After the meeting they arranged for an elaborate lunch in a local specialty restaurant, a museum tour, and a special tour to a *wasabi* (horseradish) plant. Mind you, I did not ask for these tours, since I was anxious to get home. But I ended up having to postpone my departure. I think in the future I will let them know my schedule in advance; otherwise they may arrange everything for me. (Singapore)

DISCO DISASTER
I remember I once asked to go to a disco in Tokyo. My counterpart arranged for four men and three office ladies to join us. I really did

not understand at the time why he had arranged for such a large group and why he had invited along OLs, who had nothing to do with our work team. At the disco, everyone got up and danced together as a group, the women more or less facing the women and the men facing the men. I felt very strange. Needless to say the evening ended early. I think everyone felt awkward. Now I realize that I put the Japanese in a very uncomfortable social situation. What was perfectly normal for me was not for them. You have to be sensitive to how different cultures are. (Paris, France)

HOW TO QUIT EATING

On my last trip to Japan I was invited to a Japanese home for the first time. I knew it was a special honor and so, of course, accepted, even though I'd been counting on that time to get some much-needed rest and recreation. I also had the grandfather of all headaches, but took six aspirins to help me brave it through. I bought a gift to take with me—a cake nicely wrapped—and had a great time. The only problem was that they fed and fed me until I thought I would burst. My Japanese host knew that I loved shrimp tempura. I must have eaten over twenty. I later found out that I not only ate my portion but everyone else's as well. I do recall noticing that members of the family were not eating as much as me, and food kept being put on my plate. Wanting to be polite, I kept eating what was offered. Later I found out that by cleaning my plate I was obligating the host to keep feeding me. I should have left some food on my plate to show I was full and couldn't eat any more. Since this experience I don't think I've had tempura for over a year. (Austin, Texas)

INVITED TO MY EMPLOYEE'S HOME

One of my Japanese employees, a unique individual with much experience abroad, invited me to spend a day at home with his family in Tokyo. Getting around Tokyo being the nightmare that it is, he first took me shopping for gifts for my family, then to his house on the outskirts of the city for dinner.

The house had two floors. The top floor, where the family lived mostly Western style, was about five hundred square feet; the downstairs, which was traditional Japanese style with tatami mats on the floor, was about three hundred square feet. The living room was furnished with only a TV set and a large recliner that I assumed was his. The dining room had a table with six chairs but hardly anything else. The overall effect was neat, simple, clean.

First, his wife whisked me away for a tea ceremony. She changed me into a magnificent ceremonial kimono that required tremendous wrapping, tugging, and squeezing. I could hardly recognize my own silhouette. My shapely Western self was now a curveless Japanese figurine! Then tea was served. I even liked the bitter taste.

After tea, each member of the family introduced themselves, along with their special hobby or art. The son collected butterflies, the daughter painted, the grandmother made special snacks, and my employee made tiles. He even showed me the bathroom he had tiled with his own artwork.

All in all, it was a fabulous experience, one I will cherish for a long time. (Cupertino, California)

THE KARAOKE BAR

I went to a karaoke bar once. That will also be the last time I go. The men drank a lot. As the evening wore on, the videos got more and more sexually explicit, until finally they were nothing else but gyrating nudes. The behavior of the men grew increasingly vulgar, rarely rising above the level of sophomoric sexual innuendo. I haven't put myself in that situation since. Now I only go to dinner, then back to my hotel. (Atlanta, Georgia)

HOSTESS HELL

When, after dinner, the branch manager of the Japanese firm I was visiting invited me along on a company excursion to a hostess bar, I felt some pressure to accept. Since we were going as a group, I thought it would be an interesting diversion at worst. Well, the evening turned out to be—how shall I put it?—an ordeal. The Japanese men were sexually forward with the hostesses *and* with me—in fact, I was treated like a "hostess." On top of all that, the hostesses were deliberately rude to me—I suppose from a sense of competition or embarrassment. I should have called a taxi and swiftly departed. Now I know to bow out in advance. (Detroit, Michigan)

Dos and Don'ts

❑ Japanese cities, despite their size, are safe for women. Use discretion no matter where you travel, but you don't have to worry about muggings.

❑ Tell your Japanese hosts how long you will be staying in Japan so they know how to plan (or not plan) the time. You can also assure them you will stay longer should the need arise.

❑ Advise your hosts about any serious commitments you have. Otherwise they may try to schedule all your time, day and night.

❑ Take your hotel's business card and those of the people you are visiting to hand to the taxi drivers. It is best to hail a cab from the hotel lobby.

AT DINNER

❑ Eating meals together is an important part of Japanese protocol. Plan to go to dinner the first night after your business meeting with your hosts. This is expected, almost mandatory. Do not decline the invitation.

❑ If you are visiting your staff overseas and wish to sponsor a dinner, tell them in advance about which night you prefer.

❑ If you decide to sponsor a dinner, be prepared for a large bill—about $200 to $250 per person for a nice meal.

❑ Tips are not expected in taxis and at hotels, particularly from women. However, some taxi drivers and hotel staff do gladly accept tips offered; others will politely turn them down. Service charges, if any, are added to the bill.

❑ You may be contacted by your hosts upon arrival at your hotel and then invited to meet for drinks and dinner. This will be initiated by a staff member, who will then act as your go-between during your visit. Use this pre-meeting to establish rapport and familiarity with the people you will be doing business with the next day.

❑ If you are meeting your own staff in Japan, you can invite them for drinks at your hotel the first night. This will help to establish camaraderie before you formally meet at the office.

❑ If you are not invited to dinner, you may wish to invite your guests out instead. Realize, however, that dinner will be very expensive, and you will need your hosts' help in making suitable restaurant reservations.

❑ In Tokyo dinner usually follows the meeting, and you and your hosts will travel over to the restaurant together. This is mainly due to traffic and the distances you and your counterparts have to travel. The restaurant will either be a company-associated establishment where the Japanese have an account or a local specialty restaurant.

❑ In a Japanese-style restaurant you will be seated on tatami mats. You should remove your shoes at the entrance (either to the restaurant or to your individual dining room—follow your hosts' lead). You may be given a pair of slippers to wear inside the restaurant proper, but be sure to take these slippers off before stepping onto the tatami mats. The low table at which you sit may have a well under it into which you can let your feet dangle down. Otherwise, you will begin by sitting with your knees folded beneath you. Then your host will quickly indicate that you should relax, at which point you should sit with your legs comfortably tucked to one side. Do not sit cross-legged like the men unless you are wearing pants.

❑ Dinner will have many courses, some of them unrecognizable. Do your best to try them. It is not a breach of etiquette if you do not finish what's on your plate. If the idea of raw seafood repulses you, practice in advance.

❑ Also practice using chopsticks before you go. At Japanese-style restaurants you will not be offered a fork unless you request one (even then forks might not be available). Practice makes perfect!

❑ Don't stand your chopsticks vertically in your rice between mouthfuls. This imitates an important Buddhist ritual. Instead, lay your chopsticks on the chopstick rest (it looks a small pillow).

❑ Don't pour soy sauce on your rice. Rice should remain white.

❑ Don't wash your face with the hot towel given to you at dinner. It is a hand towel.

❑ Don't slurp your soup or noodles even if men do. It is impolite for a woman.

❑ Use the unused end of your chopsticks (the end that doesn't go in your mouth) for taking food from a platter or a common dish.

❑ Don't pass food from one pair of chopsticks to another.

❑ Leave some of your drink or food unfinished to signal that you are done.

❑ Don't interrupt and debate at dinner. Wait attentively until each point is made.

❑ Don't smoke with your clients. Smoke in your hotel room or taxi. As in the U.S. years ago, smoking was for "bad" women. Today you see many younger women smoking. Many older, conservative men, however, may get the wrong idea if they see you lighting up. Hard liquor for women has a similar connotation. Sake and beer are acceptable drinks during dinner. Tea and soda waters during the day are fine (one rarely has mixed drinks at lunchtime in Japan).

❑ Only after a relationship has been established will you be invited to someone's home. This is a rare honor. Bring a gift appropriate to the occasion (see the chapter "Gift Giving").

❑ Don't be too complimentary about something displayed in your host's home. He may feel compelled by Japanese custom to give you the object.

❑ Always remember to thank your hosts the very first thing the next day for dinner the night before.

AFTER DINNER

❑ Don't use a compact, apply lipstick, chew gum, or fix your hair at the table.

❑ Don't blow your nose in public. Excuse yourself and do so in the bathroom.

❑ Politely thank your hosts, excuse yourself, and go back to your hotel. This is the best strategy for your first visit to Japan.

❑ If the group still insists you join them after dinner, an excuse such as jet lag or a pressing phone call will be quite acceptable to Japanese.

❑ Ask your hosts to help you hail a cab or have a taxi arranged to pick you up at your final destination. You may not get picked up as a foreign female as quickly as a native will.

❑ Some Western women who have established a solid working relationship with their Japanese counterparts do enjoy a nightcap after dinner with their hosts. This is entirely up to you, based on the nature of the business relationship and how well you know each other.

❑ Things may loosen up considerably once people start drinking. Remember that whatever you see and hear at night is not to be referred to at the office the next day. Sometimes, however, important information will intentionally be given to you in an informal setting. You can generally assume that in Japan people tell you what they want you to know.

❑ Do not hesitate to make an excuse and leave if you are confronted by a difficult situation.

Socializing Here

*I take dinner protocol very seriously. I think it's even more critical to business success than the over-rated and over-ritualized business meeting. I keep a list of fine restaurants that have great service, presentation, and private rooms—and I make a point of getting to know the staff. When I'm the host, I make sure to reserve a private room and a good selection of wines. I also make sure I know the chef's top specialty, so that when I'm asked for a recommendation I have an informed answer. Next I make sure to seat my guests on the side of the table farthest from the door—the place of honor for the Japanese. If the host is a woman, the Japanese will go to great lengths to pick up the tab. So I have the maitre d' hold my credit card and settle the bill later, in private. Before dinner, I make a short welcoming speech on the partnership aspect of our business relationship and on the importance of my guests' visit. Then I end with a toast—*kanpai *is the Japanese expression. And usually the highest-ranking individual in the room will answer for the Japanese side. As you can probably guess, my dinners are long and elaborate, so I don't entertain afterward. (New Haven, Connecticut)*

The rules of the game are substantially different when you entertain the Japanese here than when you are being hosted in Japan. In general, follow American dining customs. However, one important modification will serve you well on both sides of the Pacific—*be part of the dining, not the wining.*

You can do a great deal over a well-orchestrated dinner. Consider it an important part of the business relationship and a good, informal opportunity for getting to know your business partners. You can discuss business at dinner, of course, but keep it to a minimum, since that's not the point. Dining together will help build confidence in you and your team and break down any barriers that have gotten in the way during the business day. A successful dinner will help the next day's work go more smoothly. Do not, however, carry an informal and casually friendly mood of the night before into the next working day.

Given the importance of your dinner with the Japanese, you must understand the basic protocol of entertaining in order to play the proper host. Also try to make intercultural modifications in your style—speak slowly and calmly, don't dress too flashy, be on the lookout for your guests' being ill at ease or confused. Be more formal, using toasts and welcoming speeches. By doing so, you will earn a great deal of respect for your efforts and will raise the comfort level for your guests. But remember that your guests *want* to get to know you and experience your ways. Don't feel you have to take Japanese people to Japanese restaurants.

Some ideas for when you're hosting a dinner:

• Suggest a few dinner selections to your guests in order to simplify what could be an intimidating menu. If you sense hesitation over your choices, suggest they try what you are ordering for yourself. If your guests are not well traveled, prepare them for the variety of choices your waiter/waitress will rattle off (salad dressing, vegetables, etc.).

• If you are in charge, propose a toast.

• Don't let the conversation be solely about business.

• Make prior arrangements with the restaurant or excuse yourself and pay the bill away from the table.

• Treat your Japanese guests to cuisine that they don't otherwise experience (Steak House, New York Deli, Cajun, California Cuisine, etc.)—not Japanese food. At a Japanese restaurant, your guests will feel obligated to take care of you and instruct you about their food and dining etiquette, when it's you who are supposed to be taking care of them. But keep in mind that, if your guests have been traveling for some time, they may be hungry for home cooking. A nice touch is to provide them a list of good Japanese restaurants, with maps and phone numbers, and let them go off on their own for some home-style cooking.

If you are not a single woman, consider inviting Japanese to your home. In most cases, being invited to your home will be a welcome new experience for the Japanese. But because most Japanese residences are small and inconvenient for handling guests, and the occasion of having a guest in one's home in Japan is considered extremely formal, such an invitation from you can make some Japanese very uncomfortable. They may feel obligated to reciprocate in kind (a burden to them and their household), and since they are not in a position to do so they may simply make an excuse and decline your invitation. If you meet resistance to your invitation, drop the subject and choose instead to socialize at public eateries.

For your dinner, don't present too many choices, since the Japanese will feel it rude to reject an offering of food. Serve small portions, since the Japanese may not like what you serve but will feel obligated to eat it all anyway. And don't play host or hostess all night long, since this may undermine your role as a businesswoman. Arrange for someone else to do the serving, or present your dinner buffet style.

In Their Own Words

TIME CRUNCH

Picture all the year-round customer and vendor visits we get, and you'll see why I just can't stretch my working hours to include dinner each time the Japanese arrive. So I try to schedule a few dinners at the initial stages of the business relationship—to create a lasting first impression. Then, if I know it is going to be difficult for me to spend too much time away from my business and family, I apologize for not being able to join them in the evenings. I ask them to tell me what kind of food they like, and provide them with maps, addresses, and phone numbers for several good restaurants. I also write out recommended dishes at each restaurant and offer to make reservations for them. They really appreciate this. (San Jose, California)

VISUAL ARTS

The Japanese roll out the red carpet each time I visit them—all the expense and effort make me feel like a debutante. So when they come here I make a special effort to reciprocate. I take them to the ballet, baseball games (which they especially like), ice skating shows, an opera. As you can see, I keep to mostly visual forms of entertainment, in case their English isn't very good. (Oakland, California)

ON TOUR

I can't spend every night or weekend with the Japanese when they visit. I'm sure they don't want to spend every night with me either. So I do the following: For my guests' weekend activities, I rely on a local travel agency that specializes in the needs of Japanese tourists. With Japanese on their staff and lots experience, I know they'll take good care of my guests. I usually insist on at least one shopping tour as an option, since I know that the typical Japanese visitor to the U.S. has to take home a bundle of gifts. I also ask my colleagues at work to help me on open nights and take a turn at entertaining. (Seattle, Washington)

PUNCH BOWL GREEN TEA

We invited our Japanese subsidiary to our office in the U.S. Our conference rooms were fully stocked with coffee service, black tea, sodas, and juices, but one of our lawyers said that the Japanese won't drink anything but green tea and that we had better have some on hand. Naturally we had no idea how to brew the tea, and we ended up using water from the coffee machine and dumping the loose tea leaves into a big punch bowl, from which we then tried to pour the tea into little cups. This is crazy I thought, and called it off. "Trust me, the Japanese will drink coffee," I said. And they did. The next day the caterer had the bright idea that green tea probably came in tea bags. He found some bags, but he put them into coffee mugs—not Japanese teacups, which are round and without handles—and then didn't give the Japanese any place to put the tea bags when they were done with them.

It's good to accommodate your guests, but you really have to prepare in advance. It was like us going to a foreign country and them thinking you only drink milkshakes, and not even knowing what ice cream is. Learn enough so you know what you're doing. If you don't, forget it. (San Francisco, California)

EXOTIC TASTES

As a Japanese national working in the U.S., I am especially attuned to the needs of visiting Japanese. I tell my American colleagues that, if you've built up a comfortable relationship with the Japanese, they really appreciate being introduced to things foreign and exotic. Recently, I took some Japanese visitors to a Moroccan restaurant where we ate with our hands and watched a belly dancer. We all enjoyed the evening. If the Japanese are traveling alone, I try to find time on the weekends for sightseeing, golf, or shopping. (Mountain View, California)

JEKYLL AND HYDE

From the very beginning my Japanese colleague at our company seemed very contradictory in the way he related to me. I had hired him and was his boss, but he seemed not to know how to act with me. Half the time he was polite and deferential; the other half he was rude and downright insulting. And I couldn't predict how he was going to act from one moment to the next. His job was in jeopardy, and my abilities as an effective manager were in doubt. I asked the advice of a woman with a long history of success in Japan. My staff member, according to her, was suffering a classic case of culture shock. She painted the picture from his perspective: I was a female manager, alternately authoritative and friendly. My nonconservative dress, while appropriate for the firm, made it hard for him to take me seriously. His home environment had not included high-ranked professional women, so most likely he was having a difficult time adjusting to having me give him orders.

My colleague said that I had to clearly define our working relationship—make it less friendly and more formal and professional. I should have individual meetings with him to talk through business problems and try to build up a good working relationship.

Once the business relationship was established, the next step might be socializing with him on a fairly formal level. But she advised me not to invite him to my home, as this could only cause him more confusion. So that's what I did, and by keeping the business relationship primary and the socializing on a very occasional basis, my employee gradually became more comfortable with me. (Santa Clara, California)

HOMECOMING

After several years working closely with my Japanese staff, it was time to invite them to a catered party at my home. My husband and I have a large home in Arizona where we both enjoy entertaining. We also stable horses in a lot adjacent to ours. Since the Japanese are wild about horseback riding, especially Western-style, the afternoon was a monster hit. Before you try something like this, however, my advice is: (1) Know your Japanese associates very well before you invite them to your home. (2) Ask in advance if they would enjoy any unusual activity you are planning. A swim party with a female superior, for example, may be embarrassing for the average Japanese businessman and yourself. (3) Don't play the role of server all night. Arrange for someone else to take care of the catering. (Phoenix, Arizona)

Dos and Don'ts

BEFORE THEY COME

❑ Plan to host the Japanese at dinner when they visit your country. It is an expected courtesy.

❑ If your Japanese guests are visiting for only a few days, you don't have to do any more than host the first meal. Then supply your guests with necessary information for the rest of their stay.

❑ Know the hotels in your area that can cater to Japanese guests. Especially if they are staying for long periods of time they will appreciate having a Japanese breakfast and other items from home.

❑   Arrange for cars to transport the Japanese from their hotel if necessary.

❑   Plan to pay for all the entertaining when the Japanese are visiting you. They will do the same when you go to see them in Japan.

❑   Don't invite the Japanese to your home for dinner. This is not appropriate for your first few dinners, unless you are both already very comfortable with the business and personal relationship.

❑   Choose quality restaurants to entertain your guests. Popular choices are fine seafood, French, and steak restaurants.

❑   Know the chef's recommended food and wine choices. Your Japanese guests will ask for your recommendation and will usually order what you suggest.

❑   Many Japanese smoke, so you should try to find restaurants that allow smoking. If smoking is not permitted, politely advise your guests in advance so they are not embarrassed.

DURING DINNER

❑   Don't continue business discussions over dinner. This is not an appropriate topic while eating.

❑   Ask your guests questions about their culture, country, cuisine, weather, company background, holidays, favorite sports, and hobbies.

❑   Talk about local history, interesting neighborhoods, places to visit, and upcoming events in your area.

❑   Don't initiate discussions about the family of your Japanese guests. If they wish to talk about family, they will bring up the topic.

AFTER DINNER

❑ Never let the Japanese pay the bill when you are the host. They will offer out of courtesy, but do not accept.

❑ Make advance arrangements with the maitre d' to pay the bill discreetly, away from your guests.

❑ Don't leave the restaurant before your guests. Wait until everyone is ready to go and then step outside together. If you have called a taxi to take the Japanese back to their hotel, don't leave until the taxi has arrived and your guests are all safely on their way. Stand and watch as the taxi departs.

❑ The next day thank your guests for joining you for dinner. Then express the same sentiments in a brief, personal note in your next business correspondence.

❑ Don't feel obligated to entertain the Japanese after dinner. If you have provided the Japanese a list of Japanese bars and restaurants nearby, they will be able to find such nightspots and enjoy themselves without you.

Gift Giving

Our company has a policy of not giving gifts to clients, and to dis-
courage the the practice tells us we have to pay for any gifts ourselves.
If you travel to Japan as often as I do, even small gifts can add up to
quite a sum. I explained this to management, who now acknowledge
that in Japan at least gift giving is an essential part of doing business.
Even so, I don't take a gift on each trip. Instead, every once in a while,
about twice a year or so, I take a small gift—some local art or foods—
just to be polite, to balance the record, and because I genuinely like
doing it. (Palo Alto, California)

Giving gifts is an important aspect of Japanese culture that is often
underestimated by the foreign businessperson. Gifts are given on
every imaginable occasion in Japan. When Japanese travel from one
part of their country to another, they are expected to carry gifts in
both directions, first for the people they are going to visit and next for
the people they left behind at home. In the summer and winter gift-
giving seasons—occasions for giving gifts to those who helped you
throughout the year—the department stores are stacked high with
gift baskets and gift boxes of fruits, crackers, liquors, and chocolates.

Just as individuals exchange gifts in Japan, so do Japanese businesses, and on a far more lavish scale. A Japanese businessman
would never dream of going to visit you or your company without
bringing something in the way of a gift. The gift is not intended as a
bribe to persuade you to do business with him, but as a sign of goodwill between your company and the Japanese company, regardless of
the outcome of your mutual venture.

Initially, you may not want to participate in the gift-giving game. You may simply feel it is burdensome and unimportant. Or you may feel there's something unethical about the practice. But working with the Japanese you don't really have a choice. We strongly advise you to put aside your concerns and jump in head first. Appropriate, inexpensive items such as small gifts from your home state are best, since it is not the magnitude of the gift but the thought behind its selection and the ceremony of giving it that count. If you are unsure what to bring, you can choose a gift to be shared among your Japanese hosts, such as a box of chocolates or candies. Unless you specify otherwise, your gift will be opened in private. If you are the recipient, open your gift later and be sure to thank your hosts the next time you see them for their thoughtfulness. Send a thank-you note when you return home.

In Their Own Words

TIFF'D OFF

After our counterparts had visited us a few times in the U.S. and had brought us many gifts, it was finally our turn to go to Japan. I advised my management that I felt responsible for bringing the gifts. We mutually agreed that I would be funded to bring five Tiffany sterling pens since they carried our company's logo, were light to carry, had a recognizable brand name, and were a "good enough" gift. We knew that five would not be enough, but we could not bring enough pens for everyone. The pens came in individual signature blue boxes with a white bow and no wrapping, and since I was running to catch a plane I was relieved they were prepackaged. Thinking I fully understood the protocol I handed the gifts in their little shopping bag to my Japanese contact at the firm we were visiting. I explained to him that there were only five small gifts and that he should pass them out as he felt appropriate. He was quite used to Western customs, and asked the executive staff to open their gifts in front of us. I never really understood how they decided who among the group of twenty-five got the pens.

Watching the face of the highest ranked Japanese I realized something was wrong. First he held the box in his hand and stared at the bow for a while. Then he pulled it off as if it was some foreign object. Next he turned the box over looking for tape so he could unwrap the box. Eventually he just flipped the top of the box open. He smiled when he saw what was inside. The unwrapped box and the big bow were so wrong and inexpensive that he was a tad confused about the formality and the value of the gift and therefore what we were trying to communicate by giving it. If I had realized how important this simple act was I would have stopped at the airport or hotel beforehand to have the items wrapped. I never told this to my team, who thought I had done so well and who sat beaming through the whole ceremony, delighted that someone knew the protocol. (Washington, D.C.)

FASHION SHOW

It was my first trip to Japan. I was working for a large U.S. firm and was this Japanese firm's first businesswoman. I created a lot of worry and attention. We had some great dinner conversations. One of them was on traditional Japanese dress. To my delight, they described to me in great detail the various types of kimonos and costumes that Japanese women wear on various occasions. I learned a great deal and enjoyed the evening very much. The following evening I was thrown off guard when I was presented a kimono. In front of over thirty people I was asked to model the kimono. I was at a loss for words. I put on the kimono and was the center of conversation for thirty minutes. Finally I asked another woman to help me change out of it because I was so worried about spoiling the fabric that I couldn't relax. I am very proud to have received such a gift and enjoy having an authentic Japanese kimono very much. I am not sure I could advise anyone on the best way to accept this type of gift. It was completely unexpected, and while a lot more lavish than anything I was used to getting I didn't consider for a moment turning it down. Refusing the gift would have made things very difficult for my hosts. (San Francisco, California)

THE DOLL

I remember when a team from a large Japanese firm came to visit us in the U.S. We had formally awarded a project to them. I was apparently the first female they had ever worked with. Since they were a conservative company—probably the most formal and ritualistic I have met—they came in a big group with their top executives leading the way. They asked me to make some introductory remarks, so I got up and said a few words concerning our partnership and the new project. Then their head officer stood up and made a beautiful rehearsed speech in English. This was followed by a presentation of a Japanese doll in a glass case to me. The doll case had a nameplate on it engraved with both companies' names and the title of our joint project. This was one of the most creative and thoughtful gifts I have ever received. Since it was a corporate gift and not an individual gift, the doll was put in our company's front lobby case, where it adorns our entrance even today. (Cupertino, California)

STRING OF PEARLS

I remember when I was running a project for my firm with our Japanese partners. "We don't do gift giving" was company policy. I was told. I was expected to discourage gifts, and even to give them back if they were too expensive. As a last resort, we would use any gifts as company raffle prizes. On one trip, in the evening, I, as the head of the team, was handed a bag with five small wrapped gifts. They said to me, "You, as the key executive and most sensitive member on the team, will know who on your staff should receive these gifts from us. We truly appreciate all the hard work you have done on our behalf for this very difficult project. We chose these gifts with you in mind, so we hope you will receive them." The gifts were expensive pearl necklaces. I discussed my dilemma with my management and was extremely happy to hear that the policy had been modified and that my team and I could keep the gifts. The thinking here was that our policy was reasonable in most cases but not appropriate for Japan. (Chicago, Illinois)

FAN-DANGLED AGAIN

I thought I did a good job this trip of not speaking admiringly of things, not asking culturally insensitive questions, and not staying too long. I was with a Japanese firm but in Taiwan, and we were there for only a very short visit—less than a half day. But on my way out when I thought I was in the clear, a beautiful Chinese fan surfaced from under the table. Gift giving is part of the culture no matter where you are and no matter how long you stay. (Seattle, Washington)

OUR PACT

I can't keep up with all the achievements and changes in the executive staff in Japan. There seem to be a lot of promotions and transfers these days, and each such announcement occasions a gift. Since my company's relationship with our Japanese partner is a long one, we discussed gift giving and agreed to stop the gifts unless one of us told the other it was a particularly important occasion. I think this was a relief for all parties concerned. (Boise, Idaho)

THE UNWRAPPED GIFT

This happened to someone else in my company, but the story is worth retelling as a cautionary tale. My company has been working with various Japanese companies for a long time, and you think we'd be immune to such mistakes. It was a joint research and development project. A team from our company went to visit the Japanese company. We took two boxes of T-shirts as gifts for the Japanese team. True to our casual company image, the T-shirts were just stuffed into boxes and then unceremoniously distributed—unwrapped—to all the Japanese after we arrived.

Three days into the business trip the senior person from my company was politely asked, "Did you only bring one T-shirt for each person?" An odd comment, we thought, but it was soon learned that since the shirts weren't wrapped the Japanese team thought they were a uniform and had begun dutifully wearing them each and every day. At night they were going home and laundering them we assume.

Everyone in our company heard this story, and now we all wrap our gifts. (Fremont, California)

PRAISE NOT FAINT ENOUGH

I was invited for dinner to a Japanese private home. It was a wonderful evening, with good food and hospitality and conversation. During dinner, I couldn't help but notice a particular object on the wall. It was a doll made up entirely of folded paper and nicely framed. I must have kept looking at it. It was truly exquisite, and I really wanted to take a closer look. Well, soon the topic of conversation became the mounted paper doll. It turned out to be something the youngest girl of the family had made when she was only eleven.

In Japan, if you're a guest and show interest in something your host may feel obliged to give it to you. So you can guess how the evening ended. I left my host's home with the picture—only after many many attempts to refuse it. Finally I said I'd be honored to have it, and I promised to put it in my office and share it with as many people as I could.

When I got back home I put the piece in my office but still wondered what to do. Finally I decided I just had to return it. In my letter I explained that I had enjoyed the doll very much, as had the many others who had come to my office, but that I now wanted very much to return the doll to its rightful home. I said I had taken a picture of it and would be just as happy enjoying both the picture and the memories it stirred of the wonderful time I had spent as a guest in their home. (San Francisco, California)

Dos and Don'ts

Note: Gift-giving dos and don'ts in Japan are extensive. As a foreigner you need not to worry about all the subtleties. The following are the most important points.

❑ Don't bring gifts on your first trip to Japan if you are the customer, since you do not have a relationship established yet. As a sales representative you may wish to bring gifts if it is appropriate in your industry; choose modest gifts so as not to appear to be "buying" business.

❏   Bring brand-name company gifts—logoed pens, T-shirts, pins,
    golf balls, key rings, caps, tote-bags. Prestige brand names are:
    Bally, Marks and Spencer, Gucci, Harrods, Saks, Louis Vuitton,
    Christian Dior. Good brand-name items are Hermes scarfs,
    Burberry umbrellas, Tiffany pens or key rings, Mont Blanc pens,
    Cross pens.

❏   Bring brand-name liquors (especially Scotch) and wines (but not
    jug wine).

❏   Bring regional specialties: syrups, wines, candies, cookies,
    breads, cakes, art pieces. Wall calendars and books from or about
    your area are also popular.

❏   Acceptable food items are dried fruits, nuts, beef jerky, packaged
    steaks, smoked turkey, caviar, smoked salmon packages, citrus
    fruits,

❏   Ideal corporate gifts—these can be more expensive than gifts to
    individuals—include local sculpture, an engraved and dated tro-
    phy cup, Waterford crystal, Lalique pieces, Steuben glass,
    Belleek china, Royal Doulton, a sterling silver engraved bowl, a
    picture in a large sterling silver frame, or an engraved paper-
    weight. Any engraving should include the names of both com-
    panies and the date.

❏   Gifts appropriate for a home visit are a gourmet food package
    (local to your area), wine or liquor, and unusual candy assort-
    ments. Do not bring food to eat at the meal.

❏   Gifts appropriate when visiting a big group are large boxes of
    candy, beef jerky, key rings, sports caps, calendars, and T-shirts.

❏   Gifts for your subsidiary offices in Japan can be more western-
    ized items such as U.S. Disneyland souvenirs, Australian Ugg
    boots, Texas Western wear, New Zealand sheepskin, Alaskan
    Indian crafts, French perfume, Belgium chocolates, or Canadian
    moccasins. Try to pick out something that shows your thought-
    fulness and how well you know your associates, since you have
    to rely on them as your eyes and ears in Japan.

- ❑ Don't give clothing or personal items (although logoed T-shirts and sweatshirts are OK).

- ❑ Unwrapped gifts are not considered gifts.

- ❑ Good colors to wrap your gifts in are brown, maroon, blue, purple, gray, burgundy, and green.

- ❑ Don't wrap your gifts in elaborate colors such as red, orange, or gold. Don't use bows. Avoid the funeral colors of black and white.

- ❑ Don't bring flowers, since they are associated with romantic intentions.

- ❑ Don't bring gifts for your counterpart's family unless you know them very well.

- ❑ Don't give gifts in the quantity of either four or nine; these are unlucky numbers in Japan.

- ❑ Never turn down a gift. It has been pre-selected for you. If your firm does not permit gift exchanges advise your counterparts of this at the time of the first exchange. Suggest that you would like both sides to agree not to give gifts regardless of the occasion.

- ❑ Make sure your colleagues—and management—understand the importance of gift giving when working with the Japanese. They should be prepared to get gifts when receiving incoming visitors from Japan. They need not give gifts to Japanese visitors, but should be sure to take gifts when they travel to Japan themselves.

- ❑ When you arrive, hand your gift to a third party or go-between and say you have brought a gift for the group and would like it to be taken care of for you. Your go-between will most likely thank you and take your gift away without opening it in front of you. You may not hear about the gift again. More westernized firms may open the gifts in front of you and thank you on the spot.

❑ If you receive a gift do not open it in front of the giver. Thank him and put the gift away for later. Then thank your counterpart the following morning or send a note of thanks. But if you are invited to open the gift when you receive it, it is perfectly OK to do so.

❑ Some gift items to bring home for your colleagues: *yukata* or summer kimono (not too expensive, perhaps $20); an elaborate kimono with accompanying *obi* belt (very expensive; you may wish to get a used one); chopsticks and chopstick holders; lacquer dishes and bowls; *bento* boxes; sake and sake sets; tea sets; cloisonné (enameled metal in the form of jewelry); *kokeshi* dolls (no arms or legs but sometimes a moving head); *hanko* (signature seals); fans; paper wallets; stationery; woodblock prints; watches and gadgets.

❑ Some gift items to bring home for children: samurai dolls and dolls of the emperor and empress; origami kits; Daruma doll (shaped like an egg, it never falls over); games such as *go*, mahjong, tabletop pachinko, *shogi* (like chess).

Sticky Rice

At the big company dinner last year, a senior Japanese executive I hardly knew—an older man and sober, mind you—winked at me and asked "Are you hot?" I fumbled my chopsticks, looked away, and said nothing. And that's not wimping out—ignoring such pathetic remarks is, in Japanese eyes, the best way to embarrass the speaker and put you in the best light. It's the smart thing to do, especially if you want to avoid the kind of serious consequences that might destroy a valued business relationship. (New York City, New York)

Sticky, glutinous rice is a part of every Japanese meal. And the sticky situations in which Western women find themselves when dealing with Japanese men are likewise part of their daily diet. At best, these situations will make you uncomfortable. At worst, they can really gum up the works, humiliate you, and ruin the deal. The sticky-rice scenarios in this chapter are by no means intended to scare off or to discourage the American businesswoman from developing a working relationship with the Japanese. Their purpose is to share real-life incidents—some funny, some not so funny—that we have found exemplify the plight of the Western businesswoman in Japan. We hope they will help you deal constructively with some of the cultural misconceptions that can ruin what would otherwise be a happy experience in Japan. These scenarios represent a boiled-down view of "typical" Japanese attitudes that exist at all levels of Japanese society. Our experience, however, is that the ratio of enlightened to unenlightened views is the same in Japan as it is in other homogeneous societies throughout the industrialized world.

Japan, like most countries in the world, is the unfortunate recipient of Hollywood movies, *Playboy,* and Madison Avenue advertising that all portray the typical American woman as enjoying an enviably active sex life. If this is so far no different from the attitudes of the Western male—the images are, after all, of Western females—the specifically Japanese male prejudice is this: Unlike Japanese women whose behavior is constrained and whose feminine dignity is protected by the traditional, largely Confucian norms of Japanese society, whenever the Western female is not actually engaged in sex she is imagined to be talking or, at the very least, thinking about it (insatiable Western females figure prominently in the ubiquitous Japanese porno magazines). As a Western female you may be considered fair game for any Japanese male wishing to dabble in the exotic. Obviously, anything you can do to correct this perception of you as sex goddess will help ward off unwelcome attention from your Japanese male counterparts.

But this is easier said than done, and the unabashed naivete of the sexual attitudes you encounter in Japan may still surprise you. The questions directed toward you can be very personal and sexual in nature. Japanese men think that since Western women talk about sex all the time anyway, having you around is the perfect chance to talk "dirty." Whatever the cause—call it opportunism, wish fulfillment, fantasy, sexism, or cultural provincialism—read the women's stories here and prepare yourself for the inevitable "sticky situation."

In Their Own Words

MARRIED WOMEN TOO?

As an American, you'll discover that being married doesn't automatically ward off the advances of Japanese men. I recall an after-dinner meeting last year. My long-term Japanese clients and I were sharing drinks in my hotel lobby. We had broken off into small discussion groups when an another colleague of theirs I'd never met before joined our group. He watched intently as I chatted with one of my clients. During a break in our conversation, he asked quite casually if

I'd like to have sex with the client. I was speechless. After a Japanese colleague jumped in with a harsh reprimand, he promptly apologized to me. (Los Angeles, California)

UNDER THE TABLE

I think of myself as a veteran of Japanese business life. For example, when I'm asked the inevitable personal question about my life as a single woman, I just smile and say, "Let's not talk about this." I've learned that in Japanese eyes your message is most clear, elegant, and intelligent when you ward off, rather than respond to or lecture about, intrusive questions. The same is true for more direct advances. Once a man got physically aggressive with me under the table. I just stood up and said, "It's late, I have to go." When he offered to take me home I politely said, "No thanks, I can manage alone." I was firm but never got upset. The next day it was forgotten. It never happened again and the business relationship did not suffer—in short, a typical woman's experience in Japan. In general, I think the Japanese male is sensitive to the boundary between business and personal life. When he is not, he gets the message quickly. (Tokyo, Japan)

YOU WON'T BELIEVE THESE QUESTIONS!

The questions you get in Japan can really throw you for a loop if you aren't prepared. The following ones are so common they're probably required to be memorized in English class in Japanese schools. These are: "How old are you?" "How does your husband feel about your work and travel?" "Are you dating someone?" "How many boyfriends do you have?" "Why aren't you married?" "Do you plan to have children?" "Why *don't* you plan to have children?" And so on. I usually answer the questions up to a point, but I diplomatically avoid answering the more obviously inappropriate ones.

Some answers to these questions I or others have used, in order, are: "I am actually much younger than I look because my job has aged me considerably." "My husband and I both work and support each other in our careers." "Who has time to date?" "[No response]" (I don't answer boyfriend questions). "I am married to my work." "Someday." "I just haven't meet the right person to have children with yet" or "I just don't think I have enough time to have children."

I don't think you should be insulted by these questions. They are, usually, an awkward attempt to get to know you. Just hold tight and weather the difficult start. Soon the conversation will settle down to something real. (Collective responses)

DRAW THE LINE

A Japanese business associate used to follow me around when I visited Japan. He would show up at the hotel I was staying at, find out my room number, and knock on my door. It was like a child's crush. During meetings he would pout, ignore me, or get my attention by throwing meaningless insults my way. Trying to be polite, I would never come out and tell him to stop, hoping he would eventually get the message. His favorite topic of conversation was my hair. I am a natural redhead and he was fascinated by the color. Things finally popped when he asked if I had the same color hair all over my body and grinned foolishly. There was a long silence. If I hadn't learned the Japanese art of silence, I think I would have decked him. I decided to make my response short and sweet, so I said to him, "Never talk to me that way again," and left.

Patience is an important quality yes. Diplomacy I also practice. But short of a lawsuit, which I considered here, you have to draw the line and draw it fast and firm. (New Haven, Connecticut)

BREAST TALK

At a very formal business dinner in Silicon Valley, the head honcho on the Japanese team, a dignified-looking executive with graying temples, turned and for no apparent reason asked me this question: "Do you know why Japanese women have one breast bigger than the other?" Surprised but contained, I said, "No," and changed the subject. Japanese men would only talk like this to a bar hostess, never to a professional woman. All he was doing was sampling the delights of talking naughty to an American woman. I think I responded correctly. I ignored him. I could also have just stayed silent and ignored him, or even shamed him by asking one of his staff if such a conversation was appropriate to have with female professionals. (Washington, D.C.)

B FOR BOOBS, B FOR BARBARIANS

My first experience as a new hire at a Japanese firm was to have dinner with some of our Japanese counterparts who were visiting us. I was the lowest ranking person at the dinner. One of the high level executives was getting drunk. Suddenly he leaned over to one of his colleagues and said, "She has big boobs." I decided to take immediate action and told him, very seriously, that he was a barbarian. My remark was passed off as a joke, but I know it got to him, because from that day on his colleagues referred to him as "the barbarian," and I never had trouble with him again. (Fremont, California)

HIGH SCHOOL AGAIN

I am a grandmother. A young grandmother but, nevertheless, a grandmother. In my wildest imagination I could not have imagined being in a situation that I can only describe as high school silliness.

A Japanese man that I have known for six years started to act in ways that brought back memories of my adolescent relationships—if that is what you can call them. It started with hugs instead of handshakes. Then came the infamous trip to Japan. After a great deal of hugging he enthusiastically invited me to his home for dinner. I later found out from others in my office that his wife was out of town. So I politely declined the invitation. Later on, he hinted and then insisted that I postpone my flight and book the same flight as his since he was also traveling. I told him I needed to travel with my own team. Then he called me at my hotel and said, "I think you turned down my invitation because you don't want to be alone with a horny old man." My jaw dropped. So I finally had to make it crystal clear that his actions were totally inappropriate, and I reminded him that we had a professional relationship. I left it at that, which should have been enough. On my next trip to Japan he was still himself, but a bit easier to handle. Except that he did manage one bizarre act. He called my hotel room, told me he had recently broken his arm, and practically insisted that he come to the hotel for me to sign his cast.

I could swear I'm back in high school again. (Ontario, Oregon)

I ALWAYS GET ASKED

Inevitably when socializing in Japan, I get asked about my children. I reply, "I have two boys." And then the follow-up question is always "Do they miss their mother?" So I reply "Of course, and I miss them as well." Then I continue and say, "My husband is a full-time house husband [pause for the shock to register] and we made a decision a few years ago that one of us would stay home with the kids, so we worked it out that he would stay home and I would work." The usual reaction here is silence. Friends tell me that for most Japanese having children and traveling if you're a woman is quite difficult to understand. They figure something's got to give at work or at home. I have to explain how that's not the case, and that a woman can do both. (Cupertino, California)

WANDERING HANDS

Before I went to Japan a Japanese girlfriend of mine gave me a piece of good advice. She warned me that if I used the train or subway system while in the major cities—and who can possibly get around Tokyo, Osaka, Fukuoka, or any other major city without using the trains?—I would inevitably encounter "wandering hands." *The situations:* In crowded trains everyone is politely pushed and packed into the train cars so there's no space at all between you and the next person. *The problem:* In this situation, suddenly you feel an unwelcome hand on your thigh. *One solution:* The "wandering hand" phenomenon has gotten so bad that now, during rush hours, there are special cars designated for women and children only. Ride these if you can. I've lived and worked in Japan for ten years, and although I know it's a safe country this is a major irritation. (New Haven, Connecticut)

STRIPPING FOR ME

It makes a great deal of difference whether you are a customer or a vendor in Japan. Case in point. I was the customer and was in Japan to finalize the manufacturing deadlines. I was treated royally, but I had to finally draw the line and refuse the attention being bestowed on me. I was taken to a private club with private rooms, and in one room there was a couple playing strip poker. The man was asked by my host to lose more often for my sake, and he preceded to do just that. He was down to the last possible garment and was willing to dispose of it too. I, not really able to believe that this was really happening to me, said, "That's it. Enough. Please stop this game." The game stopped, we ordered more drinks and then chatted comfortably about business. (Boston, Massachusetts)

HANDS-ON ADVICE

Really, the worst thing is having to deal with the *chikan*, the train gropers. I've learned to move away, ignore, give the icy stare, and all the other things a woman has to do just to get to work in Japan. But one day I simply got fed up. Feeling a hand on my butt I grabbed it and pulled it upward, high up into the air. Then I yelled out, in English, "Whose hand is this?" Everyone turned to look, and the offender—a well-dressed Japanese salaryman—didn't know whether he should pull his hand away or simply pretend that his hand actually belonged to somebody else. I wasn't about to let go. Then, when we arrived at a station, he wrested his hand free and shot out the door. (Tokyo, Japan)

Dos and Don'ts

Note: By all means you should have a good time in Japan. But many Japanese men are simply not aware of what is appropriate behavior toward women. Our conservative recommendation is that you not put yourself in potentially difficult situations in the first place. But if you do and begin to have trouble, in most cases you should just get up and leave. Men cannot be educated in a single evening. Your departure and absence will make a significant impression on the Japanese.

❑ The most unpleasantness you will experience will involve remarks from drunkards at night and perhaps some groping on the crowded trains (in the morning even!). Ignore the drunks. Dealing with gropers is a bit more tricky. Some women simply move away. Others confront the offender and in a loud voice yell "Stop!" This usually embarrasses the culprit.

❑ Before you go to Japan, discuss with your team members what socializing you do and do not plan to participate in. It is more acceptable for a woman to bow out of after-hours events then a man. (See also "Socializing There.")

❑ Elicit help from your male colleagues if you feel harassed. Advise them to be sensitive and to take action if you're in a difficult situation. Suggest they interrupt a conversation that is going in the wrong direction or join your discussion if one of your hosts seems to be dominating your time over drinks or dinner. A word from a colleague to the Japanese side may also be in order. Men listen to men. If your hosts feel that their business might be jeopardized they will immediately stop.

❑ If you feel your team members will not be very supportive, decide at the outset to limit the amount of socializing you'll do. Many men will lapse into silence, dismiss your concerns, or join in or ignore tense situations figuring you can handle yourself. Don't let yourself be ambushed without reinforcements.

❑ If you represent a major firm and are visiting a major firm in Japan then great pains will be taken to assure that everything is done according to protocol. Anyone acting out of line will usually be reprimanded by his own colleagues.

❑ If you are a small firm and are visiting a small firm in Japan the behavior of the Japanese may be harder to predict. Don't be surprised if all is forgotten the next morning. Any bad behavior you witnessed will be dismissed as the result of too much alcohol.

❑ Be sensitive to the nature of your visit. If you are soliciting business you are in a weakened position. If you are the client or high in rank, more steps will be taken to make sure you are comfortable.

❑ Be sensitive to where you are visiting. Downtown Tokyo businesses are used to Westerners, while firms in more isolated areas of Japan are not, particularly if the Westerner is a woman on business.

❑ Go to dinner, but do not need feel obliged to spend a lengthy evening socializing (i.e., drinking) afterward. Say that you do not drink (or that you are "allergic" to alcohol—a favorite excuse in Japan).

❏ Don't encourage unwelcome conversations. Simply change the subject. Ignore leading questions. If, however, you feel the comment to you is simply beyond tolerance, be direct and say, "That is not something you may ask me. Don't discuss this topic with me ever again."

❏ Use silence. It is the most effective tool for warding off unwelcome advances and questions, and will be considered a sign of strength. Another good technique is to ignore the individual and shame him by turning to talk with someone else.

❏ Call a spade a spade and identify the bad behavior for what it is.

❏ Don't put up with anything for "the good of the business."

❏ Don't bring up personal topics, dating, affairs, divorce, etc. These are not business subjects and can lead into an awkward conversation or give your counterpart the wrong impression.

❏ If nothing else works, just leave. Ask your hosts to call you a taxi. If you don't get a response, leave the table and arrange for a taxi yourself. Your absence will be noted.

Woman Talk

I was nine months pregnant and counting when the Japanese team came to visit our company. Well aware of certain prejudices about the working woman—especially mothers—I decided to seat myself before they arrived and not stand until the meeting was adjourned. Excellent strategy. I'll never forget the look on their faces when I finally stood to escort them from the seminar room: one collective dropped jaw! (Milpitas, California)

As in business, the role of women in Japanese society at large is subordinate. But it's time to let you in on something many Japanese men don't seem to realize yet. Visible trends in the college population promise major upheavals in the sexual status quo. The ratio of marriageable men to marriageable women among the Japanese elite on college campuses nationwide is roughly one to four or five. Couple this statistic with the fact that more and more women are postponing marriage—or opting not to marry at all—and you have a major crisis for the traditional, career-oriented Japanese family man. As many surveys confirm, the shortage of educated females is already so pronounced that the Japanese male today can no longer take for granted the acquisition of an essential ingredient for any successful business career—the dutiful Japanese wife.

Along with this new status quo comes new vocabulary to match. The older Japanese wives have always had their derogatory or "leveling" terms for the class of men called husband. Among these are the old standby, *gokiburi-teishu*, or "cockroach husband" (the creature who appears after sunset and who leaves with the morning light), and the more recent *sodai gomi,* or "excess garbage" (the husband who is the biggest of the garbage). Now, however, the increasing social mobility of the educated Japanese woman, as well as her unprecedented freedom to pick and choose a mate, has given birth to an enriched vocabulary for classifying her male counterpart. For example, heard on college campuses today are such terms as:

• *messhii-kun:* "Mr. Dinner"—the man wealthy or socially presentable enough to take you out to the better dining establishments.

• *nesshii-kun:* "Mr. Sleeper"—the lover or the man with enough good qualities to stay overnight.

• *asshii-kun:* "Mr. Feet"—the man you can count on for transportation.

• *conbini-kun:* "Mr. Convenience"—the man docile enough to run errands for you.

• *mitsugu-kun:* "Mr. Finance"—the man who showers you with gifts.

• *keepu-kun:* "Mr. Keeper"—the man with enough good qualities to keep as a backup in case the others are busy.

And there is another new term. Although divorce is not as prevalent in Japan as it is in the West, the popularity of the term *Narita-rikon,* or "divorce Narita-style," indicates how this may change in the near future. The term refers to the morning-after blahs of the educated, westernized, and upwardly mobile Japanese woman who has just bid farewell to the joys of single life. This new bride, returning in shock from a week's honeymoon overseas with a groom whose "nontraditional" qualities and personal virtues she finds have been grossly oversold, calls off the marriage the moment she lands at Narita Airport.

Why is all this important for you to know? Because Japanese men's perceptions of you are guided by their interactions with Japanese women. And as Japanese women assert themselves in their society, as the language of society itself changes to accommodate their new positions of strength, you can expect Japanese men will be looking at you with increasing respect and even, perhaps, understanding.

In Their Own Words

BUMPED

Whenever I go to Japan I avoid flying Japan Airlines. I first realized I had made a big mistake when several different flight agents—wanting to be helpful, I guess—repeatedly asked me if I knew that I was standing in line for a flight to Japan. When I assured them I did, they'd invariably go on to ask if I realized I was in the ticket line for business class. That kind of attitude continued on the return flight when I was bumped from business to economy class, and "my men" were bumped up to first class! On board, the flight attendants always assumed the man sitting next to me was my husband, asked him about my welfare, and so on. Although things have gotten better, I still find that Western airlines treat women far better and I recommend them. (New York City, New York)

FANCY FOOTWEAR

There is a slipper for all occasions in Japan. If you visit a factory, home, or restaurant, you will change into slippers. In a restaurant, the slippers are either brought to you or are waiting outside the tatami room. You wear those slippers until you go to the restroom. At the restroom door—or just inside it—you switch to the toilet slippers while you use the facility. And when you leave the restroom, you'd better switch back to the original slippers or you'll have an anxious hostess following you back to your seat. (London, England)

ON PUBLIC RELIEF

You've got to be prepared to see men standing on the curbside or against a building at night and peeing right in front of everyone. The first time I saw it I was shocked and didn't really know what to make of it, especially this being "civilized" Japan and all. I since learned that it's not an uncommon practice, particularly at night after the boys have been out drinking. (Toronto, Ontario)

SAFE SEX

It's not easy finding a good OB/GYN in Japan. For the most part, women's health issues aren't talked about that much, and women aren't encouraged to get an annual check-up. It's hard to get refills if you're on the pill, since condoms are preferred and abortion is common, although neither is talked about much. Actually, they're talking about making the pill more available, but the male legislators argue that if they do everyone will start having sex and disease will spread. If a woman's going to be pregnant and traveling in Japan, she should do her best ahead of time to find out who to contact in case of an emergency. (Tokyo, Japan)

DON'T MENTION IT

More than a little excited about my pregnancy, I casually mentioned to my Japanese customers before a meeting that I was already in my fifth month. No one said a thing—you could hear a pin drop. I tried joking to lighten the mood, but nothing worked. And I was pointedly ignored throughout the meeting. My next meeting I kept my mouth shut and things went much more smoothly. (Chicago, Illinois)

THE LOWDOWN ON JAPANESE MEN

Don't be surprised by the adult *manga* (comic book) magazines that Japanese men read. They are full of explicit sex and violence, especially violence toward women—and these woman are usually drawn to look like Westerners. Some of this is just fantasy of course, since Japanese men like to fantasize about Western women. But the violence in the comics is disturbing. One explanation I have heard is that Japanese men have a mother complex. The mother is so dominant in the home that grown men use the violence in the comics to overcome and destroy her and thus reverse their power roles. And by casting the woman as a Western woman they're able to disguise their true Oedipal desires. That's what the sociologists say. (Kobe, Japan)

JAPANESE-STYLE TOILET

My first encounter with a Japanese restroom was a nightmarish experience on the bullet train. I walked in, took one look at the solitary hole in the floor, turned around and left. A quick check of the remaining toilets revealed the same, so I learned to adapt—but on a moving bullet train? And guess what—no toilet paper. In Japan, you'll usually find a Western-style toilet and a porcelain basin or hole in the floor to squat over. In major restaurants and airports you can count on at least one Western toilet. There are also co-ed bathrooms, and bathrooms with only curtains for privacy. (Portland, Maine)

JUST FRIENDS

It's not surprising to see women holding hands or walking arm in arm in Japan. One woman grabbing a friend's arm on the street is quite acceptable behavior, and is by no means to be taken as a lesbian overture. Being raised in Japan, when I moved to the U.S. I automatically took the hand of one of my girlfriends, and got an unexpected negative response. (Berkeley, California)

SWEATING IT OUT

Make sure you bring all the personal hygiene items you think you'll need, and then some. On my first trip to Japan, I had to visit several factories well off the beaten path, and on the return trip by car I unexpectedly started my period—with no shops or any conveniences for hours in any direction. I had no sanitary napkins and didn't feel comfortable asking strangers for assistance. Back at the factory, I tried to describe my problem to the receptionist. It wasn't easy, since I didn't speak Japanese and she didn't know how to play charades. Eventually she got the point and returned promptly with a pad. Much smaller than Western ones, by the way. When I got back to the hotel, I found a drug store, couldn't decipher the labels, grabbed a likely-looking pink package and hoped for the best. I knew I'd hit the jackpot when the saleswoman blushed and shoved it quickly into a brown bag. Bring everything you need. (Palo Alto, California)

Dos and Don'ts

BEFORE YOU GO

❑   Bring tissue with you. Very often public bathrooms in Japan will not have toilet paper. Also bring a handkerchief, since in Japan there is also no paper for drying your hands. You may see towels in the bathrooms in companies, but these are usually personal towels owned by female employees. Do not use these.

❑ Bring all your personal sanitary items, over-the-counter drugs, and prescription medications. These items may be difficult for you to locate and identify in Japanese stores, and they may not be the right size for a Western woman either. Carry written prescriptions too, since you may be asked to identify the drugs you're carrying at customs.

❑ Bring extra prescription lenses in case one pair breaks. Also bring extra soft contact lens solution since this is not usually available in Japan.

❑ Bring extra undergarments and nylons. Japanese women are smaller boned and shorter than Western women and you may have a difficult time finding your size.

❑ Practice deep knee bends at home for Japanese toilets. You may also wish to wear thigh-high stockings!

WHILE YOU ARE THERE

❑ Stay at westernized hotels in Japan. Many of these hotels now cater to women's needs and provide personal items in the room. Some hotels even leave special gifts and baskets for their female guests. A partial list of good hotels in major cities is in the back of this book.

❑ Use the hotel's dry cleaning services. It is usually good and efficient.

❑ The beauty parlors in Japan are terrific. You will always get a neck and head massage with your haircut, and the service is fantastic. Do it!

❑ If you are dining alone, make yourself visible in restaurant lines as the establishment may be inclined to seat the males first thinking you are awaiting a dining partner. Bring a newspaper or other materials with you to the table. This will give you something to do in case you are stared at.

❑ Don't venture out to just any restaurant if you are alone. You may become a spectator sport and be approached by curious onlookers.

❑ Don't wander around at night to quaint, picturesque, or other areas off the beaten track. You may be followed. If followed, duck into a store or turn around and face the person. He will most likely be embarrassed and walk away.

PART 2

BACKGROUND

Some Facts about Japanese Women

COMPARED WITH THE U.S.*

Average woman's salary as a percentage of the average man's
    U.S.   66%   Japan   54%

Women as a percentage of elected officials
    U.S.   13%   Japan   1%

Percentage of women in total labor force
    U.S.   44.9%   Japan   40.1%

Percentage of women over 30 who have never been married
    U.S.   13.3%   Japan   9.1%

Average number of children per family
    U.S.   1.9   Japan   1.7

Annual divorce rate per 1,000 marriages
    U.S.   21.2   Japan   5.4

Marriage rate per 1,000 people in 1960

U.S.		Japan	
1960	14.1	1960	14.5
1990	15.1	1990	8.6

Rapes per 100,000 people
    U.S.   37.20   Japan   1.40

Average age of first marriage

U.S.		Japan	
Men	25.2	Men	28.6
Women	23.3	Women	25.1

Number of births per 1,000 people
    U.S.   15   Japan   11

Age of conception (average age when women conceive)
    U.S.   23.4   Japan   26.6

Percentage of women having their first child who are over 30
        U.S.   24.2%   Japan   19.8%

Teenage mothers per 1,000 teenagers
        U.S.   54   Japan   4

Teenage abortions per 1,000 teenagers
        U.S.   44.4   Japan   5.9

Percentage of families with children headed by a single male or single female
        U.S.   Japan
        Father   3.3%   Father   1.2%
        Mother   19.7%   Mother   9.3%

Percentage of dual-income families
        U.S.   Japan
        1981   65.2%   49.4%
        1989   71.2%   52.3%

*OTHER FACTS***

Percentage of professional positions open to women in blue-chip companies in Japan: 3%

Percentage of women in managerial positions in Japan that complain of sexual harassment: 43%

Year new equal employment opportunity law went into effect in Japan: 1986

First sexual harassment case ever won in Japan: April 1991, Fukuoka Prefecture

Amount won: $13,200

---

*Statistics primarily drawn from Michael Wolff, *Where We Stand: Can America Make It in the Global Race for Wealth, Health, and Happiness?* (New York: Bantam Books, 1992).

**Business Week*, July 13, 1992.

What Some Japanese Men Think

I am an engineer and have never worked with a Japanese female engineer. On my first trip to the U.S. I stayed for three months working on a joint project. When in the U.S. I work with many women on technical issues, but I have to admit that my first feelings when I see that the technical person is a woman is "does she really know what she is doing?" Soon, though, this feeling goes away and I like the new experience. (Tokyo, Japan)

When we do business with our non-Japanese women counterparts we're never sure how much authority they really have. We believe that a man has more, but that is from our own Japanese experience. We've discovered that this is not true in the West—that their women have the same responsibilities as men. It's still very different with us. And we'll have to get used to it if we're going to be doing business with Westerners. (Hiroshima, Japan)

If a Japanese woman ever travels for her company, she is with her manager. She will not be able to answer questions about business since her manager is with her. Japanese women are not accepted as legitimate business representatives when they travel alone, whether they're in Japan or coming back to Japan for some overseas company. If a Western woman visits us here by herself, I've been told to treat her as I would treat a man. (Tokyo, Japan)

When Japanese men ask you American women questions it is usually out of curiosity about someone very exotic to us. We also have limited language ability. One of the first questions we learn when studying English is "How old are you?" So, at the first real-life opportunity, we ask it. We don't know what questions are rude to ask in other cultures unless someone tells us. Asking someone's age is common in Japan. We do not mean to insult anyone. We just want to practice our English and get to know you. (Osaka, Japan)

It may seem as if women are easily dismissed in Japan, but actually women are highly valued and have much power. Remember that the Sun Goddess who gave birth to the imperial line was female, and Japan had an empress long before the Europeans had a queen. I give my wife my entire paycheck each month, and with it she runs the household. She doesn't work, and she says she doesn't want to work. After the household chores are done, she says she prefers to pursue her hobbies and enjoy herself. (Tokyo, Japan)

Japanese men jump to conclusions about any foreign behavior that is out of the ordinary for us. For example, a Western businesswoman's reputation is subject to all kinds of rumors if she's seen walking into a hotel with a man. She becomes the target of all kinds of questions and remarks. We don't understand how rude it all sounds. (Osaka, Japan)

Divorce is still rare here and affairs are an accepted way of life, as long as they are private and don't disrupt family life. The feeling is you will meet many compatible people in your life, so why not enjoy it? Of course, I don't know if our wives would do the same. I assume not. We never ask them, but they never ask us either. (Tokyo, Japan)

Sometimes we take foreign businesswomen to karaoke bars. We really don't know what to do with our female guests. There are after-hour places that are not appropriate for women but just fine for men. The interests of the Japanese woman are all in the family. So if you're a professional woman, what can your interests be? We feel that men, no matter from what culture, have an unspoken understanding about each other. (Kobe, Japan)

We are not used to the idea of a businesswoman, so we don't know how to act around her. With time, I guess we'll learn how. We have a single woman in our department who lives alone. I wonder what she does with her spare time? Here it's not common for women to live alone. So I watch her come and go every day. It seems very odd to me. I wonder how her life is conducted. I'm not sure how to treat her in the office, how to talk to her, what her interests are, or what she's thinking. I know how to talk to the other men, but I don't feel I should talk to her the same way. (Tokyo, Japan)

Many women think of employment as a temporary situation and believe that they can always quit when things get tough. You can see why I worry about the women I manage, and why I have to keep prying about any upcoming plans for marriage. I worry that at any moment they are going to come up and announce they are leaving, and that would really make it difficult around here. (Kyoto, Japan)

Seeing a pregnant woman in the office would be very strange indeed. We really wouldn't know how to react to that. She would have to be tired all the time, and probably in discomfort too. We assume being pregnant slows you down, makes you want to rest all the time. (Kyoto, Japan)

Comment: It is said that in feudal Japan when each of the ruling shoguns received a beautiful nightingale he was asked: "And what if the nightingale does not sing as she is supposed to do?" The first shogun responded, "I will kill her." The second shogun responded, "I will teach her." The most successful shogun said, "I will wait until she is ready." Like the third shogun, most Japanese men just don't think a woman is ready for the corporate world or, worse, that a working woman is temporarily misguided and will soon pursue the rightful path of wife, mother, and homebody (the word for wife in Japan—*okusan*—literally means "person in the interior"). One of us was given the highest "compliment" by a Japanese colleague when told, "I don't think of you as woman. You have no sex." So, in the Japanese male's view of things, a successful female professional is one that is no longer really a "woman."

Many times you will not quite understand why a Japanese man asks you a certain question or behaves in a certain way with you. He is learning, and you can be a terrific teacher. Once you have established a good relationship with some of your Japanese contacts, try having an open and frank discussion on what they really think about working with you and other women.

What Some Japanese Women Think

ABOUT THEMSELVES . . .

Many Japanese women, despite what you hear, are very successful. They hold positions of prestige in the publishing, fashion, art, and design fields. They have not, however, really penetrated the hi-tech or mainstream business industries yet. Lots of women go to college and then take the OL route. They have a few years of fun, live at home, save all their money, and travel a great deal. They never get promoted at, work, of course, and usually get married and leave the company. The idea in Japan is that you cannot be a good mother and still work. (Tokyo, Japan)

Japan's Equal Employment Opportunity Law went into effect in April 1986. But I think the law actually made it worse for us. It made the career woman's hours and duties increase and become more clearly defined, but at the same time her duties at home remained a full-time job since so few Japanese men took any responsibility for housework or child rearing. Many women ended up having to choose between work and family. American companies in Japan have a healthier perspective. Japanese firms want your whole life. I ended up leaving my Japanese company and going to work for an American one. (Cupertino, California)

We women feel very isolated at the office. Japanese men don't appreciate Japanese women being aggressive and career minded. So at the company we have to be very careful about how we speak to the men—even what words we use—and how much facial expression to show. (Nagasaki, Japan)

I would like to believe the feminist movement has made great strides in the last couple decades in Japan. But young Japanese women in their early twenties from affluent families are just as traditional and conservative as they were twenty years ago. They would rather get married to what's called a "3H" man (high education, high height [i.e., tall], high salary) and live comfortably than pursue a profession-al career that offers greater choices. Such women are perfect for men in their thirties and forties who can't find women their own age. (Tokyo, Japan)

Japanese men think being a secretary is the same as having a profes-sional career job. When my company wanted to put out a PR brochure to attract applications from women graduates of top uni-versities, they asked me to pose as a secretarial assistant and take notes for the manager at a meeting. I was appalled because I was already a manager myself. But my company wasn't quite ready to present me as an image that might attract these younger women, even though I had an MBA from a top Ivy League school and had gone to an elite private university in Japan. Management seemed to be saying that a "good job" any woman could aspire to was different from a "good job" for men. You can be an office lady or "tea lady" who greets visitors, makes tea, and runs errands. You can be a secre-tary or a general clerk. Or you can be a "junior executive," which is pretty much a glorified interpreter. (Kyoto, Japan)

I'm a Ph.D. from Tokyo University and for the first five years in my company I served tea on a regular basis. I did this for two reasons. First, I didn't want to be thought of as being too different, and my degree from one of Japan's best schools made me different enough. Second, I didn't want to isolate myself from the other women in the office, for whom serving tea was expected and unavoidable. Finally, though, my role has been accepted, and I don't serve tea for the men anymore. (Tokyo, Japan)

When I was going to school the only way for a woman to get a good job in Japan was to choose one of three professions: government offi-cial, business lawyer, or university professor. The exams and educa-tional requirements for each of these professions were very tough. What I learned, though, was that although the educational system was fairly nondiscriminatory, once you graduated and looked for a job the men didn't want to hire you. I remember the college recruiters on campus wouldn't even talk to women for anything higher than secretarial jobs. Today there are laws to protect women, and appearances make you think a lot has changed. But I don't think Japan has changed much at all over the years. All the traditional practices are still going on. (New York City, New York)

Oh sure. I hired on to one of the best Japanese firms as a marketing executive since I was educated in a good school in the U.S. But all they let me do is translate documents and escort visitors. This had nothing to do with the marketing I had learned about in school. I remember when I was in school in America I got my driver's license and drove everywhere. I'd travel for days on my own. Such freedom! But now that I'm back in Japan I have to live with my parents and take on a different role. I got a great job with one of the biggest and most respected Japanese companies, but that's a trade-off for not being able to pursue my own interests and use my talents. [Note: She has since been introduced and married to a company man, and has left her firm to raise a family.] (Nagasaki, Japan)

I have lived in the States for over ten years now. I used to think I wanted to go back to Japan. I still conduct a lot of business there for my American company because I understand the culture and speak the language. At one point I was even offered a position in Japan. I went to have a look, but soon realized I could never fit in there again. I may seem quiet and reserved here, when I am compared with Americans, but compared with what I used to be I am very different. It would be too hard for me to reintegrate into Japanese society again. (Berkeley, California)

. . . AND ABOUT YOU

The American's friendly "Hello, how are you?" that doesn't mean anything is what I just couldn't stand. I'm used to it now, but when I first came to work in the U.S. I was so insulted by American women I didn't even know acting so overly friendly. They would pass me in the hall and say the usual "Oh hello, how are you" and before I could answer they'd be halfway down the hall! I'm a foreigner, and I notice that people tend to be extra friendly to me. But such artificial friendship is colder than the formal distance of my own Japanese culture. (Oakland, California)

I was shocked at American women's bathroom talk. I would go to the bathroom with another woman and step inside a stall. I would sit down and the other woman would ask me a question. I felt very embarrassed. I didn't know what to say. Talking when combing your hair is OK, but when doing very private business it is upsetting. (Detroit, Michigan)

American women should wear longer skirts and shorter slits. It is true that they are very feminine, but why do they feel they must show their feminine qualities in business? (Kyoto, Japan)

Too much touching. I think Western women touch too much. I still can't get used to the hugging and squeezing and especially the kissing. In Japan, you see women walking on the street holding hands and that amount of closeness is normal, but the more expressive affection from Western women makes me uncomfortable. (San Francisco, California)

Getting to Know Japan

Here is an edited version of Tracey Wilen's six-month account of her first experiences doing business with the Japanese. First she meets her Japanese clients at her home office. Next she goes to Japan for follow-up meetings, in Tokyo and Nagasaki. This is one woman's story, but it may be useful to you as well. Scattered throughout are some helpful Japanese words and phrases that will serve you well no matter where you go or whom you talk to, in the office or on the streets. Also included here are recommended books for you to read about Japan and Japanese business.

HOME BASE

12/1

I started working for a firm in Silicon Valley a few months ago. It's like another world. The only consistent daily event is visits from Japanese businessmen. Crowds of them show up at the company daily looking quite reserved. They are ushered into one of our large conference rooms followed by catering carts. Maybe they like to travel in groups or maybe they are attaching a vacation onto the business trip.

OHAYO GOZAIMASU.
"Good morning."

12/2

My colleague Ron was holding one of the meetings for these Japanese guests today. I asked him if I could sit in and observe too. I thought I would not be noticed in the crowd. He laughed and said, "It wouldn't be a good idea for you to sit in as an observer, since they don't know you and aren't expecting you. And since you're a woman, they would assume you're a translator or secretary."

KONNICHIWA.
"Hello" (in the daytime).

12/3

My colleague was arranging chairs at a conference room table today. He was shifting the chairs around the table from the end to the middle. He was counting the chairs, checking the lights and making sure the papers were cleaned off the tables. I went in and asked if he had decided that being a maid was a better career path. He laughed. "No. Today we are having a fairly important business meeting with the Japanese. There will be a lot of people attending from both sides, and I wanted to be sure there would be plenty of seats available." I asked him why he moved the chairs from the end of the table to the middle, picnic-table style. "In Japan," he said, "the ends of the table are not usually occupied during a meeting. The guests sit by the wall furthest from the door and the hosts sit by the wall closest to the door." "So seating is important?" I asked. "Very. And since our guests have come a long way, I try to think of things to make them more comfortable, like good lighting, comfortable chairs, private rooms, and even a separate room if they want to have an internal discussion. It's part of being a good host."

KONBANWA.
"Hello" (in the evening).

12/20

I called my friend Greg. "I am looking for a good book on Japan to read over the holidays. Can you recommend one?" "Over Christmas? Hmm, you need a good long one. Try *The Enigma of Japanese Power* by Karel Van Wolferen. It's a big book, but it traces the history and culture of Japan and takes a very critical view of how decisions are made and power wielded."

ARIGATO GOZAIMASU.
"Thank you very much."

1/1

It's New Year's. Nobody's at work in Japan until January 4 or 5. Can't get answers to any of our faxes.

OMEDETO GOZAIMASU.
"Congratulations."

4/1

The Japanese are coming to visit again. I was asked today to attend our meeting with them. I saw a fax from my company introducing me as the business member of our engineering team. "Why all the formality?" I asked. The answer: If I was not introduced by a management member, as a woman I would have no standing in the eyes of the Japanese.

SUMIMASEN.
"Please excuse me" (when entering a room) or "Thank you" (when receiving a favor from someone).

4/2

I called my friend Bruce today. We got into chatting about everything as we always do. Bruce, who had lived in Japan, would know the answers to some of my questions. Could he recommend a good book about Japan for me to read? Bruce said, "Try *Cracking the Japanese Market* by James C. and J. Jeffrey Morgan."

4/5

I received a fax today from someone on the visiting staff introducing himself to me. He outlined specific requests and ended the short note with "respond by return." I thought perhaps it was an unusual way to say "sincere regards." I looked over the fax. It had a lot of "cordial" words such as "thank you for this," "we would be honored with that," and a reference to our partnership. A colleague looked at the fax and told me I should get back to them quickly. He said that "respond by return" is the Japanese way of saying "urgent" in English.

CHOTTO MATTE KUDASAI.
"Wait just a moment, please."

But why should we respond so quickly to them when they don't always answer us so fast?

"Well," he replied, "we decide very quickly in the U.S. relative to Japan. The Japanese have been reviewing this information for months, passing it up through a series of management levels, needing to reach consensus on each decision along the way. This can take months. But once they decide, they can move very quickly, and that is what you are seeing now. They have reached an agreement internally and will move quickly on our requests."

"It seems pretty inefficient if you ask me." I said.

"We seem pretty inefficient to them too, since we all have our own different opinions. Many times they think we never think through our decisions."

4/8

I got a message today to call my contact in Japan, Mr. Tanaka. I checked the time. I guess I can't start calling them until after 4 p.m. Pacific Time to get them in their morning. This could be tough. I didn't know Japanese and I wasn't sure how good his English was. I dialed the number using the international code 011-81 for Japan and then his number. I put my card of phrases in front of me. I figured if it got tough I could say:

SUMIMASEN GA, NIHONGO GA WAKARIMASEN. EIGO GA HANASERU HITO ONEGAI DEKIMASEN KA?
"I'm sorry, I don't understand Japanese. Could I please request someone who speaks English?"

But I thought I would give it my best shot. The call got through. A woman answered.

MOSHI MOSHI.
"Hello"

MOSHI MOSHI. KOCHIRA WA WILEN DESU. TANAKA-SAN WA IRASSHA-IMASU KA?
"Hello. My name is Wilen. Is Mr. Tanaka there?

SUMIMASEN, IMA GAISHUTSU SHITE ORIMASU.
"I am sorry, he is out of the office right now."

DOMO ARIGATO GOZAIMASU. MATA O-DENWA SHIMASU.
"Thank you very much. I will call again."

I waited until 7 p.m. and tried again. After my query the woman said:

HAI, SHOSHO O-MACHI KUDASAI.
"Yes, just a moment please."

Mr. Tanaka got on the phone with a big "Hello!" At least he speaks English, I thought to myself. He thanked me for calling back. More relaxed, I casually chatted about how nice it was to talk to him. There was silence on the other end. Maybe I spoke too fast. So I slowed down my pace and spoke very clearly paying more attention to what I was saying. He acknowledged this time and answered back that it was nice to talk with me too. We kept the conversation very short. I realized that it was very easy to be misunderstood on the phone and that I should keep the detail stuff to faxes and to our upcoming face-to-face talks.

4/15
MATA ASHITA.
"See you tomorrow."

4/16
Today we had our meeting with the Japanese. The largest room in our facilities could barely fit all of us. My manager motioned to the center of the table. "Sit here," he whispered. "You are a key member of the team and they need to see this." After I introduced myself to each member, presented my card, and shook their hands, I sat down and just stared at all those faces looking at me. A curly top in the midst of male profiles. I felt fortunate that I had the insight to wear a suit—at least I matched them. My colleague had prepped me to bring a lot of business cards and to keep a stack with me. He had told me to hand the card over with both hands and accept theirs as if it was a gift. "Make sure they understand your title so you won't get lost in the crowd. And get a set translated on the flip side into Japanese for our next meeting." I collected cards and noted how the Japanese introduced themselves to our staff. They laid all their cards out in front of themselves on the table in the same order each of our members was seated in. I liked that and followed suit. I am so forgetful with names.

4/17
We had another meeting today, a long one.

KYO WA TSUKAREMASHITA NE!
"Today was tiring, wasn't it!"

Each point and question was reiterated, explained, contemplated, and then positioned from side to side. Such a slow way of doing business. I looked across the table; some of the men were dozing. How rude, I thought, not even interested in this meeting. I would never think to do such thing. There was also a lot of murmuring off to the sides. Whenever there was a point of discussion they would break off and talk in Japanese for awhile and then be silent.

MO ICHIDO ONEGAI SHIMASU.
"One more time please."

4/18

We went to dinner at a French restaurant after the meeting today. Our guests asked me what to order, so I recommended a dish. They all ordered it. Next time I will ask the chef in advance and give our guests some options.

4/19

We had a short final meeting today with the Japanese. They presented a gift to us, a beautiful doll. They invited us to Japan next month after the Golden Week vacation period.

KONDO WA NIHON E KITE KUDASAI.
"Next time you come to Japan."

I must remember to bring a gift. I wonder what I should bring. I better get a few books and take a seminar on Japanese culture.

4/22

I received a package in the mail today. Books from Bruce. Enclosed were *Japan: A Travel Survival Kit* by Robert Strauss, *Japan Solo*, by Eiji Kanno and Constance O'Keefe, the novels *Botchan* and *Kokoro* by Natsume Soseki, and *Learning to Bow* by Bruce Feiler.

4/23–24

I've just taken a very good course. A two-day seminar called "Business Communications with the Japanese." The seminar leader was Chris Brannen from BLC Intercultural in Berkeley. It was nice to take a seminar from a woman. She touched on the woman angle and the Japanese but I wanted more. I asked her if it would be different as a female. She said yes. We talked about what to wear, gift-giving, and a few potentially difficult situations. She gave me a copy of her book, *Going to Japan on Business*, to read. Based on her suggestions I bought some company logo silver pens. I wrapped them in plain blue paper without a bow. I asked her to recommend some more books on Japan. She came up with these four: *With Respect to the Japanese* by John C. Condon, *How to Do Business with the Japanese* by Mark Zimmerman, *You Gotta Have Wa* by Robert Whiting, and *Inside Corporate Japan: The Art of Fumble-Free Management* by David. J. Lu.

Interesting, I thought. No women authors on the subject.

4/29
Birthday of the late Emperor Hirohito. A holiday. The Golden Week vacation begins. No one around to answer faxes or phone calls.

5/5
Children's Day. Golden Week ends.

5/8
I am scheduled to leave today for Japan. The plane ride is twelve hours. I don't think I have ever sat still for more than an hour in my life. I am bringing all the grueling fact-finding, data back up, and support documents which I put together to prepare for this meeting. I packed my conservative business suits and an attache case as Chris suggested, and my gifts. I hope it isn't too hot. They say this is a nice time of year and the cherry blossoms may still be in bloom. I hope I can see them. I wonder if people wear kimonos as they do in the tourist books.

5/8–5/9
I know I am on a Japan-bound airplane. Smokers are everywhere, and every announcement is translated into Japanese. I picked the Japanese lunch from the menu. It looks terrible. It comes in a compartmented box. Is that seaweed?

KORE WA NAN DESU KA?
What is this?

TOKYO

5/10

We have landed at Narita Airport in Tokyo. I lost a day crossing the international date line. The airport unloading gates are jammed full, so buses are sent out to our plane sitting on the runway to bring us in. They say Narita is crowded all the time. The lines for customs and immigration are horrendous. I got my luggage, and the crowd swept me out the door.

There was a bank outside the exit. I handed them a $100 bill. I hope it is enough. I got back very little yen in paper and coin money.

Now I need to get to Tokyo. They said it was at least an hour or more away, depending on the traffic. I saw the Airport Express Bus and Airport Limousine Bus signs in front of me, close to the bank near the exit. I told the ticket clerks what hotel I was staying at. They let me use my credit card to buy a ticket and then gave me the exact time of the bus's arrival and where to wait for it outside.

I told the driver our hotel. So far so good; everyone is speaking in English. The magazine in the bus pocket said another option for getting into Tokyo is to take a train called the Narita Express. It can get to Tokyo in one hour door to door without traffic. It also services the city of Yokohama. It is more expensive than the bus. For the Narita Express, seat reservations need to be made in advance at the airport. I checked into the hotel. It took almost two hours to get here because of traffic. It was about 6 p.m. A bellboy ran to carry my luggage upstairs. I handed him some yen for a tip. He handed it back and said "No," smiled, and backed out of the room.

I was overwhelmed by the crowds. Every street looked the same, every sign was in Japanese. Everything was gray.

KOKO WA DOKO DESU KA?
"Where am I?"

I got frustrated. I got the map pointed to where I wanted to go and tried to count the blocks and direction from the hotel. I had nabbed a hotel card so I could get back. It was late and I was tired.

GANBATTE KUDASAI.
"Keep your chin up."

I asked the hotel to sign me up for the all-day tour.

5/11

Constitution Day. The bus came to the lobby, right on time at 8:00 a.m. I felt OK and not too tired. The tour guide spoke great English. The bus drove around the town and to the various sections of Tokyo. Ginza: shopping. Akihabara: electronics. Aoyama: clothing district. Asakusa: Old Tokyo. Roppongi: trendy section. Shinjuku: New City Hall. Ueno: museums. Then on to the Imperial Palace, Tokyo Tower, and the Meiji Shrine.

They took us to a Japanese restaurant for lunch. I had to take my shoes off and sit on some cushions on the floor. It is good that I am doing this today for practice. I hope I don't have to do it all week. I don't know if my suit skirts are loose enough. I will practice in the hotel. Sitting is not very comfortable. I asked the guide to show me how to use chopsticks. It was awkward. I had only practiced in that seminar I took before I left. I asked what I was eating. It looked like the food on the plane except out of the box. My guide was very kind and explained all the types of foods that I would eat while I was here.

Miso soup is a clear broth that accompanies most of meals. Miso is made by fermenting soy beans, rice, wheat, and other grains. It can be flavored with dried sardines, tofu, and Japanese radish. Each region has its own miso, and no two are the same. You sip the soup from the bowl, or you can use a spoon ladle, holding the bowl up off the table near your mouth.

Sashimi is raw fish. It is accompanied by *wasabi*, a tart horseradish, and a dish of vinaigrette. You pick up the piece of fish with your chopsticks, dip it in the sauce, and plop the whole thing in your mouth. Usually you get tuna, shrimp, a mackerel, and some more exotic things.

Yakitori consists of small pieces of chicken, beef, or pork that are skewered on a stick and cooked over a charcoal fire. It was very tasty, but I dared not ask what part of the animal I was eating.

Sushi is different from sashimi in that it is combined with sticky rice lightly seasoned with vinegar. Sushi is actually a generic term for a variety of dishes that usually include some sort of raw fish. My guide pointed out the popular types; tuna, prawn, egg, and sea eel.

There was also the familiar rolled type of sushi: white rice rolled in a dark green, dried seaweed wrapper with a filling inside. I failed miserably with the sushi as well. Fortunately we moved onto something much more approachable.

This was tempura, which is various types of fish, shellfish, and vegetables that are rolled in a flour and egg batter, fried in vegetable oil, and then served with a dipping sauce. I had no problem with this at all.

Fruit was served for dessert. They peel their grapes!

It was a nice lunch.

KORE WA OISHII DESU.
"This is delicious."

I asked my guide what other food I might be faced with during the rest of my stay.

Sukiyaki is a beef and vegetable dish that is cooked at the table in a large kettle of stock flavored with soy sauce and sweet rice wine. You select your piece of food and dip it into the soup until it is cooked to your preference. Before eating, you dip the piece into raw egg.

Shabu-shabu is very similar to sukiyaki but the meat is very thinly sliced and there are more vegetables to experiment with. You cook and dip the meat and vegetables in the same way. One sauce is usually a peanut sauce and the other a very tangy vinaigrette. After you are done the hostess will put noodles into the broth for the final courses.

Robata-yaki restaurants are reminiscent of the old way of Japanese cooking on a hearth. You order your food and tell the chef how you want to it to be cooked. The foods are displayed around the chef in front of you so you can point or ask for help if you get confused. The atmosphere of the *robata-yaki* restaurant is very lively.

Soba is a long, thin, brownish noodle made from buckwheat flour. It makes an inexpensive meal and is usually served for lunch in a broth. *Udon* is a white, thicker noodle that is made of wheat flour and is also eaten in broth.

Most meals—but not noodle dishes—will be served with a sticky white rice in a bowl. You eat the rice with your chopsticks, and you lift the bowl to your mouth, not lower your head down to the table.

The rice stays white and should not be flavored with sauces like soy sauce. The chopsticks should be placed on a small stand between courses.

5/12

A few of us figured the best way to get around Tokyo is by subway, but I need to take some time to figure out the colored map and how to match the symbols to my destinations. We will try it over the weekend. Half way down the street we tried to hail a taxi. We realized that the cabs were ignoring us and walked back to the hotel to ask for help.

TAKUSHI ONEGAI SHIMASU.
"Please help me get a taxi."

I gave the driver the business card of where we were going.

KONO JUSHO ONEGAI SHIMASU.
"Please take me to this address."

The short ride was expensive.

My colleague said at night it can become even more difficult to get a cab because there is a shortage of cabs and drivers and they can get a premium for their rides after midnight when the trains have stopped running. Usually hailers will hold up the number of fingers to indicate how much they are willing to multiply the metered fare by. He said that cab drivers at night tend to look for businessmen who are drunk and who likely live a distance out of town and will pay a premium for a safe ride home.

We arrived at the company and our host was waiting for us in the lobby.

OHAYO GOZAIMASU, YOKU IRASSHAIMASHITA. DOZO OHAIRI KUDASAI.
"Good morning, how nice of you to come. Do come in."

SHITSUREI SHIMASU.
"Thank you (please excuse me)."

DOZO KOCHIRA NI.
"In here please."

5/13

I went to the coffee shop alone this morning for breakfast. The host there smiled at me but then greeted the group behind me and seated them. The waiters all stared at me. The host came back and smiled at me again and proceeded to seat the group behind me. They were Westerners, and said to the host, "You should seat this lady first. She is ahead of us." He bowed and escorted me to a table. He was very apologetic about ignoring me. "I am so sorry. I thought you were waiting for someone." The waiters just kept staring. Was this all because they weren't comfortable that I was a female alone? Tomorrow I will eat in my room.

5/14

I gladly accepted the English translated newspaper delivered to my room with my morning room service. This was much easier than yesterday morning.

We went to the Japanese offices today for our first meeting. All industrial and gray. Nothing very new age like at home. There were large rooms with a lot of people sitting around tables all looking at each other. People were wearing uniforms. A young girl brought us tea. I tried to look at her but she kept her head down and left quickly. There were a lot of people there to greet us. I recognized some of them, others just stared at me. I took the lead and walked forward and offered my business card.

HAJIMEMASHITE. WILEN DESU. DOZO YOROSHIKU.
"Nice to meet you. My name is Wilen. It is a pleasure."

I introduced my title in the company and held out my hand. I was received very well as each person (each one a man) came up to introduce himself to me. They smiled and tried not to stare. They motioned for us to be seated. I took the middle seat just as I did in the States. This was going to be a successful meeting.

As we walked past the office to the conference room I remembered some of the reading which I did before I left.

The organization and office structure of a Japanese company has a strong Confucian influence. The basic operating units are sections, each with a chief, supervisors, and staff. Several sections make up a department, headed by a department chief. The desks are arranged in rectangles and facing each other, with the manager in the front. The department head sits farthest from the door, where he gets a good view over the department. A task is assigned to the team, and members are expected to work on the task as a team.

Sections and departments are ranked within the company. The section tables are aligned in rank order, and the more sections to a department the more important it is. In the U.S., as individuals move up in rank, their offices become larger, more walled in, and farther into the corner or the upper floors of the building, away from the staff. In Japan, workers on a team all sit facing each other and know just about every bit of business that is transacted during the day. They can also listen in on each other's phone calls. Everyone in a Japanese office knows everything about everyone.

Our hosts took us out for dinner tonight to a small restaurant that featured *shabu-shabu*. We sat at a table with a big gas burner in the middle. Beer was brought to the table. "Beer is a man's drink," they said. "Would you like some sake?" "I'll try the beer," I responded. "I hear it is very good." They laughed and asked me to raise my glass so they could pour some beer into it. "Here we pour for each other, but never for ourselves. So we must look out for each other's empty glass!" They laughed, toasted *"Kanpai!"* A long night ahead I could tell, and I was again sitting on the floor. How do they do this night after night, I wondered. One of our hosts leaned over to me and said, "If you don't want to drink all night just leave some beer in your glass. Then we know not to fill it."

5/15

There is an article in the newspaper today on new playing cards that show women in pornographic and masochistic positions. The key to the game is to collect the cards by matching the women to the scenes. The winner is the person who has the highest points. Some cards are more valuable than others. A virgin is worth a lot, and if your hand has a widow you lose points. What a warped view of life and women!

We took the bullet train today to another site for more meetings. We had to fight our way through the subway to get there. There were tons of people. For the subway we had to buy a ticket from a wall machine. Our hosts pressed the buttons for me since it was taking me too long. The trains were crowded, and people were staring at me. I might as well get used to it. The bullet train was exactly on time. It was very smoky in the car, and not a luxury liner by any means. There were women pushing carts up and down the aisle selling food in boxes, called *bento*. My colleagues told me that anything that looks sweet is probably fish, and anything that looks like fish is probably fish. Stick to *senbei*, a plain rice cracker, and you'll be fine.

We got back to the hotel rather late. The subject of dinner came up. "I want to go where I do not have to sit on the floor," I said. One person in our party checked with the concierge. He suggested a trendy new Italian restaurant. Why not? "We need to make reservations. Shall I have him do it for us?" "Nah, let's try out the phone system and see how it works." We took out our ten-yen coins and piled them up in front of a green phone and dialed the number given us by the hotel. Fortunately for us they spoke English and we managed to get a reservation. Engineers can get very testy if they don't eat.

5/16

I had some urgent news to tell my counterpart in Europe. Thinking I had the time zones under control I phoned him at his home this morning. I thought it was his early evening. After waking his wife and two young children I learned I had called him in the early morning, about 4 a.m. to be exact. I better get this straight before I upset any more people.

In the early morning from Tokyo I can call Latin America, and the U.S. In the evening I can reach Europe. Most of Asia is close to my time zone or within an hour or so.

5/17

It was my day to choose an expedition. Yesterday we went to Akihabara. Of course, traveling with all engineers, how could I not have guessed I would end up at an electronics mart where they had everything from computer circuits and wires to electronic toys and robots? This was not my idea of fun. We also went to a large toy shop and a mega-store called Tokyu Hands, where you get a twelve-page fold-out floor guide to all the departments and services. Tokyu Hands sells everything from kitchen and bedwear to sports equipment. A good place to pick up small fun items like bubble bath powder, papers, stationery, and miniature gadgets and toys of the sort you can't find at home.

Today I wanted to learn the subway system and do something more "cultural," so I decided we would go on a sumo hunt. I had read about the sumo stables where the wrestlers worked out. My guide book said the best time to grab sight of a sumo wrestler wandering the streets was at seven in the morning. So off we went before 7 a.m.. One colleague handed me a copy of the *Tokyo Transit Book* by Garry Bassin, a small white book containing every map you could ever need to get around Tokyo on the trains. "Here, if you are dragging us around you might as well make sure we get there." "Where did you find this?" I asked. "It's in every hotel lobby. Don't worry, if a sumo wrestler eats it we can find you another one." My other colleague handed me a piece of sushi that he had attached to a string like a fishing bait. "Here, you may need this too to induce one to come out of his stable."

We never did see a wrestler that day.

5/18

My colleagues went back to Akihabara today so I decided to take a Tokyo tour on a commuter boat. I got on at Azuma Bridge, which I reached on the Ginza subway line. The dialogue was in Japanese, so I had to pay attention to my pamphlet. I could see Sensoji Temple, the Ginza area, the sumo arena, the Tsukiji Fish Market, the palace garden, Tokyo tower, and other sights. At 4:30 we met at the Kabuki Theater in the Ginza section. The show was fabulous, with action, music, and beautiful costume. All the actors (male and female roles) are men. Next time I will bring binoculars so I can see better. The earphone with English-language explanations was really useful.

5/19

We are leaving today and for convenience decided to go to the TCAT (Tokyo City Air Terminal). It is located at Hakozaki, a short taxi ride from Tokyo station. TCAT is an airport ticketing and check-in depot right in the middle of Tokyo, and it helps you avoid those ghastly lines at Narita. At TCAT you can get your airline boarding pass and grab a bus right to your gate. There is a departure tax of ¥2,000.

6/4

Back home. I picked up two books at the library which looked interesting: *Empire of Signs* by Roland Barthes and *The Japanese Mind* by Robert Christopher.

NAGASAKI

6/18

Back in Japan. I have arrived at Narita and still feel overwhelmed and hot. I have to transfer to the domestic airport, Haneda, which is in southern Tokyo, to grab my flight to Nagasaki. The problem here is that getting one from one airport to another can take up to four hours, depending on traffic. I can't believe a city can be so congested. I had argued with my travel agents that four hours was an obscene layover for anyone changing planes. I checked through customs and saw the ticket booth for transfer tickets for the bus to Haneda airport. And sure enough, three hours later I arrived at Haneda.

Haneda was crowded like Narita, but a lot quieter. I had some time to kill and went over to a magazine stand. Judging by the pictures, they contained stories on sumo, gossip, fashion, food, fiction, and cartoons. There were a number of sexual scenes of women with women, women with men, and men with Western women. I was shocked. I looked at the cover again. It seemed like an OK magazine. I picked up another ordinary-looking magazine. It had the same content and all these trashy pictures. I couldn't believe they were selling this stuff on the newsstand. Then a Japanese woman walked by, picked up a magazine, and bought it. It was the one with all the sexy pictures. She just accepts this?

6/19

Nagasaki is mostly surrounded by water. I got into a taxi and pointed at a very high mountain. Not speaking English, which most don't seem to in this area, the driver just drove up there and encouraged me to get out of the car to take a look. The basin beneath me was beautiful. The waterways were full of ships. In the past this was a popular Dutch port. I pointed to a ship and the driver responded with "Mitsubishi." I wasn't sure why he said that.

6/20

I met my colleagues at the hotel, a gorgeous place. I asked at the desk. "Who's hotel is this?" They said, "Mitsubishi," and smiled. We were in the middle of downtown, and the city was bustling with activity and trolley cars riding up and down the streets. I stopped in front of a neon-lit pachinko parlor wanting to see what was inside. The room was smoky and filled with the whirring sounds of clinking balls. It was a cross between a pinball joint and a Las Vegas slot machine room. People sat by their machines, hypnotized by the action. Once in a while a player would look up with glazed eyes at us. As we walked back to our hotel I noted there were many Mitsubishi signs and billboards.

6/21

We were escorted to a very large room conference room. Oh no, I thought, this is going to be a big meeting. The only support I had been able to muster was two home base people and two colleagues from Tokyo. In walked a stately man followed by twenty others. He was obviously the highest ranked person. We had not met him in the States. Our Tokyo colleague said to me, "You lead the business card exchange with him. We will follow you." So we did the rounds. Fortunately, this time my card was translated and I had brought enough to go around. He smiled as he read the Japanese characters and introduced himself in very good English. My colleague whispered, "That was very nice of you to have your cards translated; it is appreciated here." Later he told me that the preferred translation had the Japanese written horizontally like the English. Apparently they had not used the right phonetic characters for my name. "Let me see your card before you get it printed next time. Make sure you pronounce your name for the card printer."

I returned to my seat and handed my gift to our Japanese host, telling him how much I appreciated his kindness.

O-SEWA NI NARIMASHITA.
"I am in your debt."

He handed the bag to an office girl and she disappeared. My colleague leaned over. "We don't open gifts in public."

6/22

Our hosts took us to a memorable tea ceremony this evening. I remember trying to memorize every move made by the women in kimonos. The tea ceremony, they told me, had been introduced to Japan from China. It was perfected in the sixteenth century as a ceremony based upon the spirit of Zen.

The key to the ceremony is a calm state of mind and simplicity, although the procedures themselves are quite elaborate. A woman in a kimono with an elaborate belt called an *obi* spoons the tea leaves into the cup, pours in the hot water, whisks the tea, and then hands it to the guest.

They asked one of my colleagues to be the recipient of the tea. This role goes like this: You pick up the tea cup in your right hand and place it in the palm of your left hand. Then you rotate the teacup three times with your right hand. Drink the tea and eat the little cookies. After you drink the tea, use your right hand to wipe the area on the cup where you have sipped from. Rotate the cup counterclockwise and return it to the hostess.

The room we were seated in to watch this ceremony was sparsely decorated and had an outstanding view of Nagasaki. We sat on tatami mats as we watched. Afterward women in kimonos sat down next to each of us. This was a very uncomfortable experience for me, since my hostess spoke very little English and giggled a lot. She was very young and had obviously served only men in this restaurant before. She did see me shifting uncomfortably on the tatami mat, where I was seated kneeling on my legs. She motioned to me to unfold my legs into the well under the table. That was a relief. We didn't chat very much since we had a severe language barrier, but she kept filling my drink glasses with samples of hot and cold sake and beer just in case I wanted to drink what the men did.

After dinner cars were outside waiting to take us to another place. I asked a colleague where we were going. To a hostess bar, he said. It was late and I did not wish to have more ladies giggling at me. I was with all men and it seemed like an odd place to go late at night. I jumped in a car with a close colleague and said, "Tell the driver I feel ill and to take me to the hotel. Tell our hosts I have important phone calls to make." I wonder if that was the right thing to do.

SHITSUREI SHIMASU.

"Excuse me" (when you are leaving).

6/23

KINO NO YORU WA DOMO ARIGATO GOZAIMASU. TOTEMO TANOSHIKAT-TA DESU.

"Thank you for last night. it was very enjoyable."

I asked my colleague how the night before had gone. "Long and tiring and more of what went on at the table," he said. "Better for you you got some rest." I mentioned how beautiful the restaurant had been. He said that when he had said the same thing last night the Japanese told him it was owned by Mitsubishi. In fact, they said, Mitsubishi owns a lot of this town.

The Japanese are staring at me. It is very quiet. They're wondering why I left last night. I whispered to our go-between: "I am so sorry I couldn't go on with everyone last night. I felt the group would feel more comfortable since I was the only woman." He nodded knowingly and said something in Japanese to the group. They smiled and nodded. The meeting began.

We needed to have a serious decision made, one that would require more expertise and data collection from the home base. We had expected a business-only meeting, but R&D issues kept creeping into the discussion. There was a lot of murmuring going on at the table on our host side.

"Can you tell what they are saying?" I asked my Tokyo colleague.

"I gather that they don't feel you have the authority to make the decision that's needed today, and since it's a serious situation they're making plans for coming to the States to visit with your headquarters."

I was upset. No authority?

The problem was we needed to get an engineering sample back to the States and reviewed by internal staff. "Well then," I said to my colleague out of earshot of the Japanese, "we will have to get a decision made by the team here. First, you send your assistant back to Tokyo with the engineering data and a sample this afternoon. He is to review it with the engineers in your office. They should then send a fax analysis to my engineer in California by morning Pacific time, and call him to answer any questions. They are to make him feel as if he has the sample in his hands."

I then wrote out instructions for my engineer. I told him to meet with the staff at the home base and go over all the data provided by the Tokyo office. Together they were to make an R&D recommendation, and fax that to my hotel room later this evening with the data and analysis as to how they had come to that decision. I would present the findings on the following day.

My Tokyo colleague was shocked but followed the instructions. Off went our assistant to Tokyo with the sample. All we told our counterparts was that it was imperative he return to Tokyo today. We carried on the rest of the business meeting.

I got my phone call that evening. "The fax has already been sent to you with our analysis." I got the fax sent up from the lobby, and together the rest of the team and I went over it point by point. By 3 a.m. we had come to a conclusion. In the morning I used the hotel's business center to draft a formal letter with my signature and make copies to the appropriate staff.

6/24

We went back to the meeting room this morning. I am glad this trip is almost over as I am exhausted. It is tedious coming here day after day. I passed my colleague the fax and asked him to have the Japanese secretary make enough copies to go around. We had our usual greetings and sat around the table. It was our day to summarize and close. I cleared my throat and mentioned that we would like to open a discussion on the engineering sample and data. I passed the documentation provided to me from the home base. I reviewed point by point our decision and the plan we wanted to follow. I handed my go-between the letter. Someone on the Japanese side stood up in disbelief. A few just huddled and reviewed the documents. Then someone clapped. There was excitement in the room our team could feel it. Each member got up and shook our hands in relief. A decision was made in the eleventh hour.

We summarized the week's events and prepared to leave. I stepped out to go to the ladies room and an engineer caught my glance. "You have our respect," he said, and he bowed.

6/25

I am the last one here. Everyone has left. My hosts are very kind.
They don't like me being here alone. A car is going to come at 8:00
a.m. to pick me up at the hotel. A woman from the marketing department is to take me around town. Why are they sending a woman I
don't know to show me around?

The marketing woman arrived as scheduled. She was young and
very bright. She had gone to college and lived in the U.S. for a few
years. She said how much she missed the freedom she had had in the
States. She was supposedly in marketing, but her main job was to
escort visitors. Do the males in the marketing department escort visitors? No. She shrugged and said Japan is very slow to change.

We visited a Shinto shrine and then went to a beautiful garden
park. Also owned by Mitsubishi. We were rushing to get to the airport,
but managed to stop at the park built to commemorate the atomic
bombing of Nagasaki. It was very painful for me. Everything was
very quiet.

My guide helped me pick out a special pound cake in the airport
to bring back home. "This is a very good cake and is only made in
Nagasaki. It originates from the days when the Dutch lived here."

IROIRO DOMO ARIGATO GOZAIMASHITA.
"Thank you for all you have done."

PART 3

DETAILS

Basic Tips before You Go

❑ You only require a passport to visit Japan. There are no required vaccinations.

❑ Make and confirm all your appointments in Japan before you go. Cold calling to prospective clients will not work.

❑ Japan is very expensive. Most purchases in Japan are still made in cash, but you can use your credit card at almost all hotels and at most good restaurants (all major cards are accepted, and the rate depends on the day the transaction is posted). Take lots of traveler's checks, denominated in either dollars or yen depending on how you think the exchange rate is moving.

❑ There is a bank in the airport. This is a convenient place to exchange money. Exchange rates at hotels will be higher.

❑ Wear comfortable clothes and drink a lot of water on the plane as the flight to Japan will likely be a long one.

❑ Don't bother with an international driver's license. You don't need to drive in Japan. There is plenty of good and convenient public transportation.

❑ Book all your hotels in advance. Do not wait until after you arrive in Japan. If you don't know a good hotel (see the list in this book), ask your hosts to recommend one that is close by to their offices and convenient to transportation.

❑ If your team is arriving at different times and from different places, arrange to stay in the same hotel. This makes it easier for your hosts to arrange for pick ups and drop offs.

❑ If your hosts are arranging your group's transportation, stay somewhere close to where you plan to have your meetings with them. Traffic is very heavy on city streets, and during morning and evening rush hours the trains will be packed with commuters. If you have a secretary, interpreter, or third-party office, have them take on the role of arranging transportation. If you must transport yourselves around town, pick up a map before you set off and decide your route so that you won't be late.

❑ If you need an interpreter, find one through your subsidiary if you have one, or ask your hotel to recommend an agency. Hire your own interpreter; do not use someone who is provided by your hosts, since they may discover privileged information or fail to interpret for you accurately. For less critical business, most Japanese firms will have someone attending the meeting who speaks English, so in many cases an interpreter is unnecessary.

❑ Reconfirm all your flights and hotel reservations before you go. Make sure that if you have to transfer flights from the international Narita Airport (northwest of Tokyo) to the domestic Haneda Airport (south of the city) you allow three to four hours of travel time. Then if you're lucky and get to Haneda in good time, you can switch to an earlier domestic flight instead of sitting around the airport.

❑ If you arrive at Narita Airport and do not have pre-arranged transportation to Tokyo you can take a taxi (very expensive, about $180), bus, or train to downtown. Allow about two hours door to door.

❑ If you arrive at Narita and need a local flight from Haneda Airport you will need to take the transfer bus or go by train or taxi. Public transportation is much cheaper and often just as fast as a taxi.

❑ Your hosts may ask your flight itinerary so they can arrange transportation from the airport to your hotel. If this is your first trip to Japan you should enjoy this courtesy rather than trying to figureout your own way to your hotel.

Correspondence Protocol

Most of your day-to-day communication with Japan will be by fax. One of the biggest frustrations when sending a fax to Japan is the amount of time it sometimes takes the Japanese side to reply. Remember that in Japan there is often no single person in charge of decision making; you may have to wait for a weekly committee meeting before getting a reply. Also, the Japanese may hesitate to send you a fax in English without having the wording checked by the resident "English expert." During holiday times in Japan—such as around New Year's and mid-summer during the Obon festival—there may be no one at all who can answer your questions or provide you with information. Be patient.

In this section are some tips for writing faxes and letters that will be clearly understood and make a good impression.

SUGGESTED FORMAT

❑   Use company letterhead.

❑   Put the full name and title of the recipient on the header.

❑   Opening statement: Put any thank yous and apologies here

❑   Body of the letter: Use bullets or outline form.

❑   Closing statement: emphasize your mutual relationship.

❑   Your name, title, and signature.

❑   Attach data and diagrams on separate sheets.

OTHER TIPS

❑   Your faxes and letters can be very short and to the point, but always frame them with a greeting and closing. Start with a warm-up statement like "Thank you for your last visit" or "It was good to see you again" that recalls your most recent interaction.

❑ Don't announce bad news in the first sentence.

❑ End your letters with a statement like "I look forward to our continued relationship."

❑ Consider using only your initials to sign your correspondence, so that the Japanese will not be aware that they are dealing with a woman. Otherwise, they may mistakenly assume you are a clerk/assistant and that your request is a low priority. This strategy can be useful especially if your work is conducted only through fax and letter writing, or if you are at the initial stage of your business relationship.

❑ When writing the name of the recipient, use the English "Mr." It is usually not wrong to use -san as in "Tanaka-san," but if the person has a senior title such as Director, using -san instead of the title could be considered rude or demeaning. Using the English honorific avoids this problem. Some Japanese women will write to you and call themselves "Miss" or "Mrs." (rarely "Ms."). Follow their lead.

❑ Japanese read English very well but may not understand complicated sentences, questions, slang, double negatives, idioms, or "difficult" words.

❑ Try to have someone at your office reread your important letters to be sure they convey what you intended in the clearest way possible.

❑ Send a copy of the letter to the appropriate team members on both sides.

❑ Copy an upper management person on both sides if you feel your letter may be left unanswered. Don't use this strategy too often, or the senior person will start to ignore your requests.

SAMPLE FAX/LETTER

January 15, 1993

To: Mr. Akira Tanaka
       Marketing Director
       Parts Division
       Nihon Super Tools

From: Chris Thompson
       America Enterprises

Re: request for marketing reports

Dear Mr. Tanaka:

It was nice to see you last week and to have dinner together. I hope all is going well with your busy schedule now that the New Year is here.

Please send us two items:

    1. The Nihon marketing plan for Super Tools for June 1993.

    2. The Nihon distribution plan for Super Tools.

Please also send to America Enterprises:

    1. Nihon's 1992 marketing summary for Super Tools.

    2. Nihon's segment growth study for 1992–1993.

I will call you next week on Thursday, January 21 at 9:00 a.m. your time to discuss these matters with you.

Perhaps we can have the general meeting in Tokyo this year.

I look forward to speaking with you.

Best regards,

Chris Thompson
Director of Marketing

Business Seating Charts

AT A MEETING

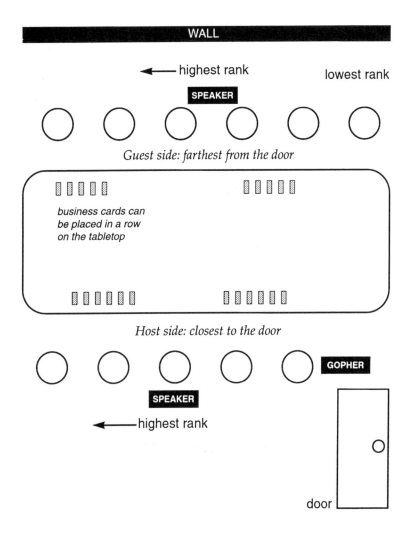

WALL

← highest rank   lowest rank

SPEAKER

Guest side: farthest from the door

business cards can
be placed in a row
on the tabletop

Host side: closest to the door

GOPHER

SPEAKER

← highest rank

door

AT A JAPANESE-STYLE DINNER

DECORATIVE ALCOVE

highest rank

Guest side: farthest from the door

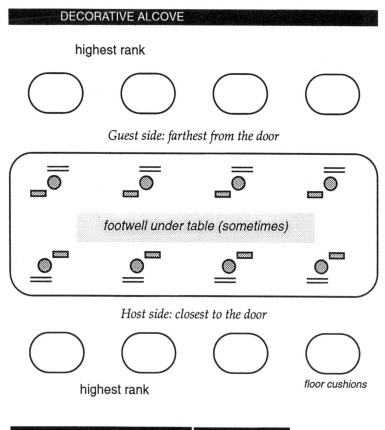

footwell under table (sometimes)

Host side: closest to the door

highest rank

floor cushions

SLIDING SCREENS

*slippers are left outside
a Japanese-style room*

AT A WESTERN-STYLE DINNER (YOU ARE HOST)

| VIEW | | VIEW |

highest rank

SPEAKER

Guest side: farthest from the front of the room

Host side: nearest to the front of the room

toward
cashier

AT A WESTERN-STYLE DINNER WITH ROUNDTABLE SEATING (YOU ARE HOST)

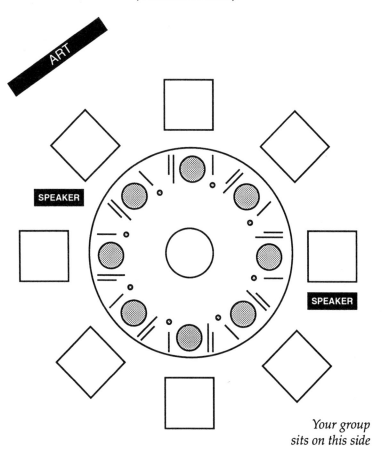

*Your group
sits on this side*

toward cashier ➤

About Business Cards

Business cards are important in Japan of course, but there is a great deal of myth surrounding the "proper protocol" that relates to them. The following is a checklist of everything you must know and do when exchanging business cards with the Japanese.

BEFORE YOU GO

❏ Make sure your name and title are translated into Japanese on the reverse of the English side. You can have this done before you go for about half the price of doing it in Japan. Pronounce your name to the printer over the phone—or write it out phonetically—to make sure the correct phonetic characters are used to represent its pronunciation.

❏ Give your card to everyone.

Exception 1. When meeting the president or CEO of a Japanese company, you present your card only if the Japanese executive gives you his/her card first.

Exception 2. If you are the president/CEO, it is not necessary to give your card to everyone. Everyone already knows who you are. Ask your Japanese staff to advise you as to who should get your card.

WHEN GIVING YOUR CARD

❏ Have your cards ready to present. Put them in the side panel of a purse or briefcase where they are easily found. Place them in a card holder so they stay clean and crisp.

❏ A women is expected to be more courteous that a man. You should present your card holding it with both hands.

❏ Present the card English side up (you should have English on one side and Japanese on the other) with the words on it in the direction of the receiver. The Japanese will want to try to read the English, and by giving them the English side you are complimenting their language ability.

WHEN RECEIVING SOMEONE'S CARD

❏ Receive it with both hands whenever possible.

❏ After receiving someone's card, study it carefully and confirm the pronunciation of the giver's name and his/her title.

❏ Do not put the card away too soon. Hold it in the palm of your hand, and when the meeting starts, place the card (and any others you've received) in front of you, face up on the conference table.

DURING THE MEETING

❏ Refer to the business cards during the meeting. Getting people's names correct is very important.

❏ It is OK to write on someone's card. You will hear people tell you it is disrespectful and that you should jot down information on a card only after the meeting when the giver is not present. This is usually impractical and, worse, produces mistakes—it is much more important to have critical information on a person correct and at your fingertips. (Example: During the meeting you may learn that Mr. Ogawa spent time at UC Berkeley, traveled extensively throughout Europe, speaks Spanish, or has a daughter at school in Canada. This information is important and should be noted on the business card he gives you.)

❏ When the Japanese talk among themselves during a meeting, take this opportunity to memorize faces and names and titles. By getting this right in the beginning you will enhance your negotiating position.

AFTER THE MEETING

❏ Pick up all the business cards you've received and put them away in your briefcase.

❏ Do not leave anyone's business card behind.

❏ Sort through the cards later to reassociate names and faces. Be sure to bring the cards to your next meeting (you do not have to display them, however; always carry a good supply of your own cards too, since the Japanese may very well introduce new people at subsequent meetings).

Getting Help in Japan

If you are having a problem related to sexual harassment in the U.S., find out first if your own company has any procedures for dealing with complaints. Remember that Japanese companies in the U.S. are required to follow U.S. law. American companies operating in Japan are also supposed to be run according to U.S. antidiscrimination laws. Needless to say, at Japanese-owned companies in Japan the situation is much more difficult, not only because the company is foreign but you are too. You may feel pressured or isolated. If you are faced with sexual harassment in Japan, some of the groups listed here may be able to help you out, providing emotional support and advising you as to what your next step should be. (Note that when calling from within Tokyo you do not need the prefix 03).

❑ In any emergency dial **110** to get the police. Speak slowly in English.

❑ Fire or ambulance service is **119.**

❑ To find a doctor, probably your best bet is to ask at your hotel, which will have English-speaking physicians on call. **St. Luke's International Hospital** in Tokyo (03-3541-5151) and the **Osaka University Hospital** in Osaka (06-451-0051) will also handle English-speaking patients.

❑ It is best that you bring prescription drugs in advance, but if you run out, try the **American Pharmacy** at the Hibiya Park Building, 1F, 1-8-1 Yurakucho, Chiyoda-ku (tel: 03-3271-4034). It is near Yurakucho Station and the Ginza shopping district.

❑ Your first call in any kind of personal crisis should be to **Tokyo English Life Line (TELL).** Trained counselors answer the phones and provide an ear to listen, or they will refer you to other specialists or organization. Their number in Tokyo is 03-5481-4301.

❏ **Kaisha Society** is for foreign employees of Japanese companies. Contact Ivy Silveman in Tokyo at 03-5487-2404 (fax at the same number).

❏ **Foreign Executive Women (FEW)** is an association of women working in Japan for both foreign and Japanese companies. For information in Tokyo, call Hannah Sorscher or Jackie Vosburgh at 03-5466-9121.

❏ The **Rape Crisis Center** of Tokyo has people who speak English. Call them at 03-3207-3692 on Wednesday from 7 p.m. to 10 p.m. or Saturday from 3 p.m. to 6 p.m. Outside these hours, leave a phone message.

❏ Referral for sexual harassment complaints will be made by the **Foreign Resident's Advisory Service**, in Tokyo, at 03-5320-7744.

❏ Another helpful group is the **Asian Women's Shelter (H.E.L.P.)**, established primarily for exploited Asian women. In Tokyo, call them at 03-3368-8855.

❏ **International Feminists of Japan** meets once a month. Contact them in Tokyo by calling Makiko Deguchi at 0423-97-5609 (fax at the same number).

❏ An American woman who has become a Zen priest in Japan offers instruction in meditation and help in coping with day to day problems in Japan. Contact **Ann Jiho Sargent** in Tokyo (Toshima-ku area) at 03-3940-0979.

❏ In Osaka you can contact the **Women's Center Osaka** at 06-933-7001. They offer general counseling and health services. They request that calls in English be made to Ms. Uno on Tuesday, Thursday, Friday, or Saturday between 10 a.m. and 5 p.m.

❏ Lesbian support groups: In Tokyo call **Suzanne Robinson** at 03-3336-6755. In Osaka, call **Barbara Bull** at 078-991-5295.

❏ A women-only bar is **Mars Bar** in Shinjuku 2-chome, open from 6 to 12 p.m. daily. English-speaking customers are welcome. Call them at 03-3354-7923. Pricey, but you are encouraged to linger.

As a woman on business you are best advised to avoid the more quaint-looking Japanese-style inns (called *ryokan* or *minshuku*) and opt for the larger Western-style "international" hotels. Japanese-style lodgings generally lack business amenities, and the English ability of the staff may be very iffy. Also, a woman staying alone in such a place would be considered rather odd. There are many inexpensive "business hotels"—often near the train stations—but these also lack amenities and are populated exclusively by males. Since these business hotels are very reasonable in price (¥7,000 per night versus two or three times that amount in the "better" places), you should not reject them out of hand, but be cautious. If your clients won't know where you are staying they can be a good choice. However, if your clients will be picking you up and looking after you during your stay, you should definitely choose the more up-scale establishments. Any of the ones listed here will be fine. Note that outside of Tokyo, Osaka, and Nagoya there aren't many luxurious Western-style international hotels. Your travel agent will be able to provide you with current prices, reservations, and more suggestions.

TOKYO

ANA TOKYO
1-12-33 Akasaka, Minato-ku
Tokyo 107
Tel: 03-3505-1111
Fax: 03-3505-1155
900 rooms, 33 suites, 25 executive rooms. Very centrally located. Business center, presentation facilities, jogging track.

CENTURY HYATT
2-7-2 Nishi-Shinjuku, Shinjuku-ku

Tokyo 160
Tel: 03-3349-0111
Fax: 03-3344-5575
800 rooms, 20 suites, 39 executive rooms. Located in western Tokyo near New City Hall. Business center, secretarial services, computers, presentation facilities.

FAIRMONT
2-1-17 Kudan-Minami
Tokyo 102
Tel: 03-3262-1151
Fax: 03-3264-2476
208 rooms, 3 suites. Near Imperial Palace moat on quiet tree-lined street (beautiful during cherry-blossom season in early April). Limited business services.

FOUR SEASONS
Chinzan-so Gardens
2-10-8 Sekiguchi, Bunkyo-ku
Tokyo 112
Tel: 03-3943-2222
Fax: 03-3943-7339
300 rooms. Very fancy. Spectacular gardens and fine dining on old aristocratic estate. A bit inconvenient to commercial districts and subways.

HILTON
6-6-2 Nishi-Shinjuku, Shinjuku-ku
Tokyo 160
Tel: 03-3344-5111
Fax: 03-3342-6094
808 rooms, 45 suites. Business center, conference center, secretarial services. Tennis courts and fitness center. Near New City Hall in western Tokyo.

IMPERIAL
1-1-1 Uchisaiwai-cho

Tokyo 100
Tel: 03-3504-1111
Fax: 03-3581-9146
1,140 rooms, 76 suites. Shopping boutiques, business center, health club, conference facilities, courtesy van to airport. Near Ginza and commercial district. Very prestigious.

NEW OTANI TOKYO
4-1 Kioi-cho
Tokyo 102
Tel: 03-3265-1111
Fax: 03-3237-3707
2,057 rooms, 1187 suites. Lovely 10-acre garden in the heart of downtown Tokyo, near government offices. Business center, conference center, secretarial services, fitness center.

OKURA
2-10-4 Toranomon
Tokyo 105
Tel: 03-3582-0111
Fax: 03-3582-3707
888 rooms, 101 suites. Near Kasumigaseki and American Embassy. Business center, conference center, secretarial services, health club. Acclaimed for its dedication to service and elegance.

TAKANAWA
2-1-17 Takanawa, Minato-ku
Tokyo 108
Tel: 03-5488-1000
Fax: 03-5488-1005
132 rooms. Good choice for access to southern Tokyo area.

TOKYO PRINCE
3-3-1 Shibakoen, Minato-ku
Tokyo 105
Tel: 03-3432-1111
Fax: 03-3434-5551

484 rooms, 17 suites. Near Shiba Park, Tokyo Tower, and Roppongi entertainment district. Business center, conference center, secretarial services.

NAGOYA

NAGOYA MIYAKO
4-9-10 Meieki, Nakamura-ku
Nagoya 450
Tel: 052-571-3211
Fax: 052-571-3851
400 rooms, 2 suites. Near main railway station and business district.

NAGOYA TOKYU
4-6-8 Sakae, Naka-ku
Nagoya 460
Tel: 052-251-2411
Fax: 052-251-2422
568 rooms, 15 suites, 88 executive rooms. Near city center. Business center, conference center, secretarial services, fitness center.

HILTON-NAGOYA
1-3-3 Sakae, Naka-ku
Nagoya 460
Tel: 052 212-1111
Fax: 052-212-1225
453 rooms, 26 suites, 28 executive rooms. Near city center. Business center, conference center, presentation facilities, secretarial services, computers, fitness center.

OSAKA

HILTON-OSAKA
1-8-8 Umeda, Kita-ku
Osaka 530

Tel: 06-347-7111
Fax: 06-347-7001
527 rooms, 39 suites, 44 executive rooms. In the city center, very modern, with all suites in Japanese style. Business center, conference center, secretarial services, fitness center.

NEW HANKYU
1-1-35 Shibata, Kita-ku
Osaka 530
Tel: 06-372-5101
Fax: 06-374-6885
1,249 rooms, 37 suites, 2 executive rooms. In city center. Business center, conference center, secretarial services, presentation facilities. Fitness center, jogging track.

NEW OTANI OSAKA
1-4-1 Shiromi, Chuo-ku
Osaka 540
Tel: 06-941-1111
Fax: 06-941-9769
574 rooms, 47 suites, 87 executive rooms. Near Osaka Business Park, Osaka Castle, and museums. Shopping arcade. Business center, conference center, secretarial services, computers.

NIKKO OSAKA
1-3-3 Nishi Shinsaibashi, Chuo-ku
Osaka 542
Tel: 06-244-1111
Fax: 06-245-2432
655 rooms, 8 suites, 60 executive rooms. Deluxe accommodation near city center. Business center, conference center, secretarial services.

ROYAL
5-3-68 Nakanoshima, Kita-ku
Osaka 530
Tel: 06-448-1121
Fax: 06-448-4414

1,200 rooms, 51 suites. All Japanese style. Near city center. Business center, conference center, secretarial services, presentation facilities. Fitness center, jogging track.

KYOTO

WESTIN KYOTO TAKARAGAIKE PRINCE
Takaragaike, Sakyo-ku
Kyoto 606
Tel: 075-712-1111
Fax: 075-712-7677
322 rooms, 28 suites. Across from Kyoto Conference Hall. Business center, jogging track.

KYOTO GRAND
Shiokoji-sagaru, Horikawa, Shimogyo-ku
Kyoto 600
Tel: 075-341-2311
Fax: 075-341-3073
560 rooms, 14 suites. Near main station. Revolving restaurant with view. Conference center.

KYOTO ROYAL
Sanjo-agaru, Kawaramachi-dori, Nakagyo-ku
Kyoto 604
Tel: 075-223-1234
Fax: 075-223-1702
331 rooms, 15 suites. Conference center.

MIYAKO
Sanjo Keage, Higashiyama-ku
Kyoto 605
Tel: 075-771-7111
Fax: 075-751-2490
366 rooms, 10 suites, 40 executive rooms. Eastern Kyoto. Beautiful traditional inn accustomed to international visitors and executives.

NAGASAKI

NAGASAKI GRAND
5-3 Manzai-Machi
Nagasaki 850
Tel: 0958-23-1234
Fax: 0958-22-1793
125 rooms. Conference center.

NAGASAKI PRINCE
2-26 Takaramachi
Nagasaki 850
Tel: 0958-21-1111
Fax: 0958-23-4309
183 rooms. Only two years old, and a short walk from the station.

SAPPORO

SAPPORO PARK
Nishi 3-chome, Minami 10-jo, Chuo-ku
Sapporo 064
Tel: 011-511-3131
Fax: 011-531-8522
227 rooms, 4 suites. Downtown. Business center. Jogging track.

SAPPORO GRAND
Nishi 4-chome, Kita 1-jo, Chuo-ku
Sapporo 060
Tel: 011-261-3311
Fax: 011-231-0388
585 rooms, 8 suites. Downtown. Conference center.

SENDAI

TOKYO DAI-ICHI SENDAI
2-3-18 Chuo, Aoba-ku

Sendai 980
Tel: 022-262-1355
Fax: 022-265-2890
154 rooms. City center. Conference center. Some business services.

SENDAI TOKYU
2-9-25 Ichiban-cho, Aoba-ku
Sendai 980
Tel: 022-262-2411
Fax: 022-262-4109
302 rooms, 3 suites. Near city center. Conference center.

Index

ABOUT THE AUTHORS

Bilingual and bicultural, Christalyn Brannen lived in Japan for twenty years and was educated in both Japanese and American schools. She is a partner in BLC Intercultural Business Consultants of Berkeley, California, which provides training and consulting for American and Japanese businesses both in the U.S. and abroad. She is also author of *Going to Japan on Business: A Quick Guide to Protocol, Travel, and Language* (Stone Bridge Press).

Tracey Wilen is a Supply Base Manager in International OEM Imaging Operations for Apple Computer, Inc., of Cupertino, California. She works closely with Apple's Japanese hardware partners and conducts her sourcing activities mainly with international firms in Asia and Europe. Before joining Apple, Tracey worked in advertising media sales for major consumer publications in New York City. She holds an MBA degree from San Jose State University.

For a complete list of other
Stone Bridge Press publications
on Japan and business, contact:
STONE BRIDGE PRESS
P.O. Box 8208
Berkeley, CA 94707
tel 510-524-8732 • fax 510-524-8711
CompuServe 71650,3402